FREDERICK DOUGLASS
AND THE
FIGHT FOR FREEDOM

MAKERS OF AMERICA

FREDERICK DOUGLASS AND THE FIGHT FOR FREEDOM

DOUGLAS T. MILLER

Facts On File Publications
New York, New York • Oxford, England

Frederick Douglass and the Fight for Freedom

Library of Congress Cataloging-in-Publication Data

Miller, Douglas T.
  Frederick Douglass and the fight for freedom/Douglas T. Miller.
    p. cm. — (Makers of America)
  Bibliography: p.
  Includes index.
  Summary: Traces the life of the black abolitionist, from his early years in slavery to his later success as a persuasive editor, orator, and writer.
  ISBN 0-8160-1617-8
1. Douglass, Frederick, 1818-1895.
2. Abolitionists—United States—Biography.
3. Afro-Americans—Biography. 4. Slavery—
United States—Anti-slavery movements.
[1. Douglass, Frederick, 1818-1895. 2. Abolitionists. 3. Afro-
Americans—Biography. 4. Slavery—Anti-slavery movements.]
I. Title. II. Series: Makers of America (Facts on File, Inc.)
E449.D75M54 1988
973.8′092′4—dc19
[B]
[92] 87-28806

Printed in the United States of America

10 9 8 7 6 5 4 3 2

Series design: Debbie Glasserman

For Sus, Edith, and Henning

Portrait of Frederick Douglass attributed to Elisha Hammond. The National Portrait Gallery, Smithsonian Institution.

CONTENTS

ACKNOWLEDGMENTS

T hanks are due to my friend, colleague, Afro-American scholar, and tennis partner, Harry Reed, for his perceptive reading of the entire manuscript. David Blight, former student and fellow Douglass scholar, and Tony Scott, my editor, also carefully read this work and made many helpful suggestions. Here in Holland, where I am spending a pleasant year as the John Adams Professor of American Civilization at the University of Amsterdam, the manuscript has further benefited from the close scrutiny of my friends Robert Twombly and Eduard van de Bilt.

Throughout the writing of *Frederick Douglass* my wife, Sus, has been a constant help and encouragement. She read and reread each chapter, discussed Douglass with me on numerous occasions, and was always ready with good advice. To her and her Danish parents this book is dedicated.

Douglas T. Miller

Singel Canal, Amsterdam, The Netherlands
January 27, 1988

1

THE EARLY YEARS

The young slave slept fitfully. Lying on the clay floor of a small kitchen storage closet, huddled in a coarse corn sack for warmth, he was aroused by voices. One was angry and shouting; the other voice, a woman's, was desperate and pleading. Peeking through a crack between the rough-sawn boards, the now awakened boy beheld his Aunt Hester stripped naked to the waist standing on a stool, her arms stretched above her with her wrists tied together and secured to a hook in the ceiling joist. Though the man's back was toward him the frightened boy recognized at once his master, Captain Aaron Anthony. With horror he watched as the man rolled up his sleeves and commenced beating the young black woman with a heavy, yard-long whip made of strips of dried oxhide. Vile curses, loud cracks, and heart-rending screams filled the night air. Blood dripped from the girl's back. Blow after blow fell on the poor slave until finally the old Captain, with a last savage oath, lowered the whip and slumped exhausted.

To the terror-stricken, seven-year-old slave boy this inexplicable and sadistic beating left a lasting impression. "I never shall forget it whilst I remember any thing," he later wrote. "It was the first of a long series of such outrages, of which I was doomed to be a witness and a participant. It struck me

Woodcut showing a slave mother being lashed as she is separated from her child.

with awful force. It was the blood-stained gate, the entrance to the hell of slavery through which I was about to pass."

This whipping occurred in the spring of 1825 and was the boy's first recognition of the true horror of slavery: its cruelty, its arbitrariness, the absolute authority of the master and the way such uncontrolled power corrupts. "The slaveholder, as well as the slave," he would later reflect, "is the victim of the slave system." There was another lesson the lad would later learn: the sexually exploitative nature of slavery. Hester, the boy's aunt, was an exceptionally attractive 15-year-old girl. Her crime consisted of rejecting the advances of her old master.

The small child who witnessed this brutal beating carried the long name of Frederick Augustus Washington Bailey. Remarkably, though raised in bondage, he would educate himself, escape from slavery, and, under the name of Frederick Douglass, become an internationally renowned reformer, a major voice in the fight against slavery, a great orator, a newspaper editor, an adviser to presidents, a high officeholder, and the recognized leader of the American Negro. Few figures in American history have led lives so eventful, dramatic, and significant as Frederick Douglass.

Despite his incredible success, Frederick Bailey, like most slaves, was born in obscurity. Throughout his life he was never able to find out his precise birth date. From circumstantial evidence he judged it to be around mid-February 1817. Only recently has research uncovered a written record revealing Frederick's birth to have taken place in February 1818. The exact day is still unknown. Because his mother on her last visit brought him a heart-shaped cake and called him her valentine, he chose to celebrate his birthday on February 14th, Valentine's Day.

Of his mother, Harriet Bailey, Frederick knew little. "I never saw my mother, to know her as such, more than four or five times in my life; and each of these times was very short in duration, and at night. She was hired by a Mr. Stewart, who lived about twelve miles from my home. She made her journeys to see me in the night, travelling the whole distance on foot, after the performance of her day's work. She was a field hand, and a whipping is the penalty of not being in the field at sunrise." Even what little comfort the young slave boy derived from his mother's few visits soon ended. She died when he was about seven. So indifferent were slaveowners to the family feelings of their slaves that the child was not allowed to be present during her illness, at her death, or burial. "She was gone long before I knew any thing about it," he sadly recalled.

But if, as Frederick later remembered, he had "very scanty" knowledge of his mother, of his father he knew nothing. One of the boy's great regrets was that his mother had died without leaving him the slightest intimation of who his father was. It was common knowledge that he was a white man. Though Frederick's mother was quite dark, Frederick was light-skinned. Rumor had it that the boy's master, Captain Aaron Anthony, was also his father. Certainly this was quite possible. White masters not infrequently had sexual relations with their female slaves, as Anthony had attempted with Hester. But if the Captain was Frederick's father he never acknowledged it. By both law and custom the children of slave women were treated as slaves regardless of who the father was. This was done, according to Frederick's later analysis, to administer to the slaveholders' lusts "and make a gratification of their wicked desires profitable as well as pleasurable." For a slave the "penalty for having a white father," Frederick claimed, was harsh treatment: "a man who will enslave his own blood may not be safely relied on for magnanimity."

While Frederick knew little or nothing about his parents, the boy was not without a strong sense of family and place. Separated from his mother at infancy, he was raised by his maternal grandparents, Betsey and Isaac Bailey, whom he later described as "the greatest people in the world to me." Isaac was a free black who worked as a sawyer, cutting lumber and firewood for white plantation owners. His wife, Betsey, though a slave, was allowed great freedom. She lived with Isaac away from the slave quarters and had as her main duty to her master, Captain Anthony, only the care of her many children and grandchildren until they became old enough for plantation work. Isaac and Betsey were industrious, independent, and caring. Their little log cabin on the banks of Tuckahoe Creek in Talbot County on Maryland's Eastern Shore was a place of enchantment for young Frederick. Here he spent the first six years of his life surrounded by siblings, cousins, and loving grandparents. It was a carefree existence. Frederick would recall the joys of exploring the woods and streams, fishing in the mill pond, drawing water from the well, and climbing a ladder to the sleeping loft he shared with the other children. "Living here, with my dear old grandmother and grandfather," he wrote later, "it was a long time before I knew myself to be a *slave*."

The idyll of Frederick's early childhood, however, was not to last. He came to learn that he was something called a "slave" and that there existed a powerful someone named "Old Master." Then one day late in the summer of 1824 Betsey alternately walked with and carried the six-year-old boy some 12 miles to Captain Anthony's farm. There she left him. Shocked by the separation from his beloved grandmother and his "first introduction to the realities of the slave system," Frederick cried himself to sleep.

The duties assigned the boy were not arduous. Considered too young to work in the fields, his tasks consisted of such things as keeping the chickens out of the garden, cleaning the yard, driving cows to and from the barns, and running errands. Neither overworked nor physically abused, Frederick was soon witness, nevertheless, to slavery's harsher realities. It was here that he watched Captain Anthony's flogging of his Aunt Hester.

This was not the only violence the slave child observed. On another occasion he saw his badly beaten cousin Betsey begging the master for protection from a drunken overseer. Though blood streamed from open gashes on her face and back, Frederick heard the master order her to return to the overseer, shouting that if she wasn't quick about it he would "take off the rest of her skin himself." Young Frederick particularly remembered the brutality of an overseer named William Sevier. His name was pronounced "severe," and, as Frederick noted, he "was rightly named: he was a cruel man. I have seen him whip a woman, causing the blood to run half an hour at a time; and this, too, in the midst of her crying children, pleading for their mother's release. He seemed to take pleasure in manifesting his fiendish barbarity."

Even more frightening than whippings to Eastern Shore slaves was the prospect of being "sold down to Georgia," a term that blacks used in reference to any slave sale to the Deep South. The possibility of being transported hundreds of miles, never again to see his friends, relatives, and the familiar land of his birth was a nightmare that haunted young Frederick. Some slaves were sold for disciplinary purposes. Frederick's cousin Betsey, for example, was sold to an Alabama slave trader soon after she complained to the master.

Economic factors, however, caused most slave sales. During the colonial period Maryland's Eastern Shore region had developed a profitable plantation economy based largely on tobacco. But by the early nineteenth century tobacco prices were down and its long planting had greatly reduced soil fertility. Wheat, corn, and cattle were increasingly introduced to offset declining tobacco production. Yet because this proved neither as profitable nor as labor intensive, many slaveholders found themselves with an excess of slave labor. However, while Maryland and much of the upper South experienced depression, the expanding new cotton kingdom of the Deep South created an insatiable demand for slave labor. As a consequence slave traders from the lower South became a common sight on the Eastern Shore.

For blacks these changed economic circumstances created frightening uncertainties. As bad as slavery was, at least when tobacco was profitable generation after generation of slave families lived, worked, and died amidst familiar people in the place of their birth. Frederick Bailey's family was typical in this respect. Before his birth there exists no record of any member of the Bailey family ever having been sold off the Eastern Shore. The economic hardships afflicting the upper South in Frederick's generation changed all this. In his first 14 years Frederick's sister, two aunts, seven cousins, several other relatives, and numerous blacks whom he knew well were sold to the Deep South, and disappeared without a trace.

But if being "sold down to Georgia" was a constant dread, it was also a spur to escape. By Maryland law, killing a runaway slave was perfectly legal. Yet though the risks were great, hundreds of Eastern Shore blacks attempted to flee to the North, and some succeeded. That there were "free states" and that escape was possible was a revelation to young Frederick. In late August 1825 Frederick's Aunt Jenny, his mother's younger sister, and her husband, Uncle Noah, both of whom belonged to Captain Anthony, managed the flight to freedom. Though only seven at the time, Frederick later recalled that their escape was "the first fact that made me seriously think of escape for myself. . . . Young as I was, I was already, in spirit and purpose, a fugitive from slavery."

Even as a child Frederick was a keen and sensitive observer, and there was much about slavery that seemed wrong to him. It was not just the violence or the threat of forcible separation from families and friends, it was the whole slave system. One thing especially affected young Frederick: the difference between the life-styles of masters and slaves. His own master, Captain Anthony, lived comfortably, though not pretentiously. In addition to owning 30 slaves and about 600 acres, Anthony also served as the chief overseer for Colonel Edward Lloyd V, and the Anthony house where Frederick served was very close to Colonel Lloyd's palatial mansion called Wye House by the whites and simply "the Great House" by the blacks. Three-time Maryland governor and twice United States senator, Colonel Lloyd was one of the wealthiest and most socially prominent men in America. His home estate and surrounding farms encompassed some 10,000 acres tended by more than 1,000 slaves. His stables of racing, saddle, and carriage horses had no equal. His gardens and orchards, planted with exquisite flowers and fruits from around the world, were among the most notable in the nation. To keep slaves from stealing fruit, the Colonel had the garden fences painted with tar. Any slave caught with tar marks was whipped. Colonel Lloyd was famous for his elaborate entertainments. "Immense wealth, and its lavish expenditure," Frederick observed, "fill the Great House with all that can please the eye, or tempt the taste."

The contrast between the opulent life at the Wye House and that at the nearby slave quarters could not have been greater. At Wye elegantly dressed ladies and gentlemen feasted at tables laden with such delicacies as fresh crabs, oysters, terrapins, wild ducks, geese, pheasants, venison, choice beef, veal, lamb, and, from the plantation smokehouse, famed hickory-cured hams and bacon. Fine wines and brandies from France and Madeira were offered along with teas from China and coffee from Java.

Close by, slave children like Frederick ate skimpy portions of boiled corn meal called "mush." As Frederick described it, the mush was poured in a trough and placed on the kitchen's dirt floor. "The children were then called, like so many pigs, and like so many pigs they would come and devour the mush

. . . . He that ate fastest got the most; . . . and few left the trough satisfied." Many times Frederick found himself so hungry he even fought Old Nep, the dog, for scraps and crumbs.

In addition to being almost constantly undernourished, Frederick also remembered being cold in winter. His yearly clothing allotment consisted of only two coarse linen shirts that barely reached his knees. No shoes, socks, or trousers were provided; nor was he given a blanket or bed. In an effort to keep warm, he stole a bag that was used for carrying corn to the mill. "I would crawl into this bag," he recalled, "and there sleep on the cold, damp, clay floor, with my head in and feet out." On several occasions his feet became frostbitten. In later life they were badly cracked because of this. Such hardships very early on led Frederick to see the extreme injustice of a system where blacks did virtually all the labor and received nearly nothing in return, while white slaveholders such as Colonel Lloyd lived in a princely fashion made possible by the toil of slaves.

While Frederick grew restless in bondage, he kept his feelings to himself. To his master and other whites he appeared as a model slave. Keen of intellect, pleasing in personality, attractive in appearance, on several occasions in his young life Frederick was singled out by whites for favors or special service. One of the first to be captivated by the boy's charms was Lucretia Anthony Auld. Lucretia was the pretty daughter of Captain Anthony and the wife of Thomas Auld, the captain of Colonel Lloyd's sloop. She took a liking to Frederick and sometimes gave him bread and butter, especially when the boy sang for her. Once she cleaned and bound his bleeding forehead cut in a fight with another slave. Frederick never forgot her kindness; it was the first he had received from a white person.

The young boy also impressed the wealthy Lloyds. Though he was not owned by Colonel Lloyd, arrangements were made to have Frederick serve as a companion to 12-year-old Daniel Lloyd, the Colonel's youngest son. The two boys became playmates and friends. With Daniel as a guide, Frederick got to explore the vast Lloyd estate. He learned in detail of the entertainments at the Great House. Through Daniel he gained insight into the elaborate world of wealthy white plantation owners. A natural mimic, Frederick also learned to imitate the aristocratic speech patterns of his playmate. This association with Daniel led Frederick very far from the world of the slave quarters and served as one more stimulus to his desire for freedom.

In early March of 1826 Frederick was once more selected for special service. He was to be sent to live in Baltimore with the family of Hugh Auld, the brother of Captain Anthony's son-in-law, Thomas Auld. Frederick had already heard fascinating descriptions of the great city from Daniel and some of the Lloyd slaves. On March 18, excited at his new prospects, the eight-year-old Frederick Bailey, well scrubbed and wearing his first real pair of trousers and shoes, set sail on Colonel Lloyd's magnificent sloop, the *Sally Lloyd*. As the ship rounded Long Point on its way into Chesapeake Bay, Frederick took a last look at the Great House. He would not see it again for 55 years, by which time slavery itself and the whole way of life represented by Colonel Lloyd had ended. When Frederick finally returned to Wye House it would be as a guest.

The next morning the *Sally Lloyd* put in at Smith's wharf in the bustling city of Baltimore. By the late 1820s Baltimore had become the third largest city in the United States. A major seaport, its docks could be seen piled high with wheat, corn, and tobacco from the plantation; sugar, molasses, and rum from the West Indies; teas, spices, and silks from the Orient; and various manufactures from England and Europe. Sailors from many ports roamed the streets. Local industries also flourished and none more than shipbuilding, which centered in the Fells Point district. Here, various shipyards produced the world-famous Baltimore clippers—some of the fastest and most graceful ships ever built. Hugh Auld, Frederick's new master, worked as a carpenter at one of the shipyards. Later Frederick, too, would find employment in the yards, first as a common laborer, then as a skilled ship's caulker.

Frederick's first task on arriving in the city was to assist in driving some of the Colonel's sheep to a nearby slaughter-house. Then one of the ship's crew led him to his new home

Baltimore, Maryland, about 1830. From a contemporary painting that shows the harbor docks, warehouses, steamboats, and sailing craft.

on Alliciana Street in the Fells Point district. There he was warmly received by Hugh and Sophia Auld and their two-year-old son, Tommy, who was to be Frederick's charge. Mistress Sophia appeared particularly sweet to the slave: "Her face was lighted with the kindliest emotions; and . . . the tenderness with which she seemed to regard me . . . greatly delighted me, and lit up, to my fancy, the pathway of my future."

Quickly taken in as part of the family, that evening for the first time in his life Frederick sat at a real table and ate a proper meal of meat, cornbread, and milk. After supper he was shown to his own bedroom; instead of the cold dirt floor he now had a straw bed and ample covers. Frederick's first impressions of his mistress proved true, and he came to regard "Miss Sopha," as he called Mrs. Auld, as "more akin to a mother than a slaveholding mistress. . . . So far from deeming it impudent in a slave to look her straight in the face, she seemed ever to say, 'Look up, child; don't be afraid.'" This was a valuable lesson for the young man.

Living in the city during the formative years of his childhood had a major effect on Frederick's life. Urban slavery was very different from bondage on the plantation. In the city there were no overseers like the dreaded Sevier terrorizing brutalized groups of field slaves. Being in the great minority, urban slaveholders' treatment of slaves had to be more in keeping with the moral values of the community. As Frederick later noted: "He is a desperate slaveholder who will shock the humanity of his nonslaveholding neighbors, by the cries of the lacerated slaves."

The very occupations of urban slaves as a rule gave them far greater freedom than on the plantation. The typical city slave worked either as a household servant or as a laborer. Household servants like Frederick generally were treated as family, while laboring slaves worked the same hours and under much the same conditions as free workers. In Baltimore, too, free blacks outnumbered slaves. This in itself made a mockery of the slaveholder's common contention that slavery was the natural state for blacks.

Such opportunities as urban life provided were rare on the plantation. Little wonder then that Frederick, looking back later on, would come to regard his removal from Colonel Lloyd's "as one of the most interesting and fortunate events of my life." City life gave him a vision of freedom that he never lost. "Going to live at Baltimore," he wrote, "laid the foundation, and opened the gateway, to all my subsequent prosperity." So significant were the Baltimore years to his future triumphs that he would subsequently refer to his being picked to go there as "a special interposition of Divine Providence."

Frederick took full advantage of his new urban opportunities. Most notable and important was his extraordinary feat of teaching himself to read and write. His desire to become literate was first awakened one Sunday evening soon after he had come to live with the Aulds. Hearing Miss Sopha reading aloud from the Bible, her voice "mellow, loud and sweet," he thought how wonderful it would be to be able to read. "The next day, I asked Mrs. Auld to teach me to read.

She consented, and soon taught me the alphabet and to read words of three or four letters."

When Sophia Auld shared her pleasure at the boy's rapid progress with her husband, Master Hugh was furious and demanded that his wife stop teaching Frederick immediately: "If you give a nigger an inch he will take an ell [about 45 inches]," Hugh told her. "Learning will spoil the best nigger in the world. If he learns to read the Bible it will forever unfit him to be a slave. He should know nothing but the will of his master, and learn to obey it. . . . If you teach him how to read, he'll want to know how to write, and this accomplished, he'll be running away with himself."

Her husband's speech had a marked effect on Mrs. Auld. Never again in the seven years Frederick remained in her household did she offer him any more lessons. Her very character changed; from the "most kind and tender-hearted woman" Frederick had known, he sadly saw "her noble soul overthrown," until "she finally became even more violent in her opposition to my learning to read, than was her husband himself."

While Hugh Auld's words strongly influenced his wife, they had an even more profound impact on Frederick Bailey. If knowledge unfitted one for slavery, then knowledge was precisely what he most desired. "From that moment, I understood the pathway from slavery to freedom. . . . I was gladdened by the invaluable instruction which by the merest accident, I gained from my master. Though conscious of the difficulty of learning without a teacher, I set out with high hope, and a fixed purpose, at whatever cost of trouble, to learn how to read." Come what might, Frederick became determined to take his "ell" and more. Against his master's and mistress's will, he embarked upon the incredibly difficult course of obtaining an education. To shed the ignorance that was the badge of slavery, then, was his first struggle against the system, his first struggle for freedom.

2

FROM SLAVERY TO FREEDOM

Forbidden lessons at home, denied access to school, Frederick found his classrooms on the streets. Already friendly with a number of neighborhood white children, he quickly managed to make them his teachers. Many of these youngsters were from poor families and often went hungry. Frederick, who was now well fed, found that in exchange for a piece of bread he could get them to share their lessons with him. On other occasions he obtained help through trickery. By the time Tommy Auld was in school Frederick had been sent to work in Master Hugh's shipyard. There he learned to write certain letters by observing the carpenters, who would initial various ship timbers to designate their use. Having mastered a particular letter Frederick would approach his street friends and proudly chalk that letter on a fence board and say: "Let's see you beat that." The boys, of course, would then write various other letters which Frederick would quickly memorize. "During this time," he later recalled, "my copy-book was the board fence, brick wall, and pavement; my pen and ink was a lump of chalk." Soon he obtained a *Webster's Spelling Book*, which he secretly carried with him everywhere. He also sneaked looks at Master Tommy's schoolbooks when the Aulds were out. By adopting these various strategies, within a few years Frederick could both read and write.

Finding reading material was another problem, however. Prohibited books at home, he scoured the streets for any scrap of newspaper or other printed matter. In this way he first learned that there were people called abolitionists who were working to end slavery. He found out more about the free states. He also read of Nat Turner's August 1831 slave rebellion in neighboring Virginia. Turner, a slave possessed of personal magnetism and great intelligence, led a slave uprising that was not suppressed until some 57 whites were dead. Though this event terrified and enraged the slaveholding South, to Frederick it seemed divine retribution. Other reading matter he came across consisted of pages of the Bible and a Methodist hymnbook.

Hugh Auld had been right: the more the boy read and learned, the more resentful he became of slavery. Knowledge that he was a slave for life became an almost intolerable burden to him. Often he discussed slavery with his white playmates. "Have I not as good a right to be free as you have?" he would ask. Such questions troubled his white friends. Indeed, throughout his years in slavery he never met a young white person who defended the slave system. He came to the conclusion that "nature never intended that men and women should be either slaves or slaveholders, and nothing but rigid training long persisted in, can perfect the character of the one or the other."

At the age of 13, Frederick, having earned 50 cents shining shoes, bought his first book, a secondhand copy of a widely-used school text called *The Columbian Orator*. The book consisted of short speeches by renowned orators praising temperance, honesty, courage, diligence, liberty, freedom, equality, and democracy. There were addresses by such famous people as George Washington, Cicero, Socrates, Charles Fox, and William Pitt. Frederick read their eloquent words over and over. He was particularly impressed by Daniel O'Connell's moving appeal for Catholic emancipation in Ireland. He interpreted this as "a bold denunciation of slavery, and a powerful vindication of human rights."

The book also contained bits of dialogue for students to memorize. One of these was an exchange between a master and a slave in which the slave finally convinced the master of the immorality of slavery and his duty to set him free. The more Frederick read the book the more he detested slavery. He now regarded slaveholders as "a band of successful robbers, who had left their homes, and gone to Africa, and stolen us from our homes, and in a strange land reduced us to slavery."

The Columbian Orator confirmed Frederick's belief in human equality, but it also deepened his discontent. He was still a slave. The book had given him a view of his wretched condition, without a remedy: "It opened my eyes to the horrible pit, but no ladder upon which to get out." So great was his despair that he almost envied other slaves their ignorance.

During this time of emotional turmoil over his enslavement Frederick experienced a religious conversion. Long concerned with fundamental questions about the nature of the universe and why he was a slave, the 13-year-old boy began to listen more seriously to the teachings of local Fells Point preachers, both black and white. The sermons of a Reverend Hanson, a white Methodist, first awakened Frederick's religious awareness and convinced him that great and small, slaveholder and slave, were equally sinners in the eyes of God. Then influenced by a black lay preacher, Charles Johnson, he began to seek salvation through prayer. After experiencing weeks of torment and doubt, at last he found faith: "that change of heart which comes by 'casting all one's care' upon God."

The 1830s were a great period of religious revivals throughout the United States, and Baltimore was no exception. Numerous whites and blacks experienced conversions. Though some slaveholders were wary of allowing slaves to become Christians, others hoped religion would make them more accepting of their fate. The message most white preachers offered to blacks was one of resignation and acceptance of their lot. They taught that slavery was the benevolent creation of God and that faithful and obedient slaves would be rewarded in heaven.

Blacks such as Frederick Bailey interpreted Christianity very differently. To them it meant the equality of all people before God and deliverance from bondage in this life. Religion taught Frederick to value himself, to love others, and to work to achieve freedom. His religious faith was life affirming and gave him both comfort and a degree of personal autonomy. Through religion, he wrote, "I finally found my burden lightened, and my heart relieved. I loved all mankind, slaveholders not excepted, though I abhorred slavery more than ever." In his later years he would have little use for organized religion because of the hypocrisy of too many professed believers who both went to church and supported slavery. Nevertheless, throughout his life Christianity's ideals helped inspire his work and guide his actions.

While in the flush of his conversion, Frederick met a devout, elderly, free black named Charles Lawson who became his "spiritual father." The saintly old man and the eager young slave were constant companions. They read the Bible together, went to prayer meetings, and attended the black Methodist Bethel Church that Frederick had joined. One night Charles Lawson had a vision that he revealed to his friend: The Lord had chosen Frederick for great work that he must prepare to do. When the boy questioned how he was to accomplish this mission as a slave, the old man assured him that "if you want liberty, ask the Lord for it, *in faith*, AND HE WILL GIVE IT TO YOU." This thought filled Frederick with new hopes and intensified his already strong love of knowledge and desire for freedom.

Frederick had only a short time to enjoy his newfound religious fellowship with Lawson and the other members of the Bethel Church. In late March 1833, with no say in the matter, he was removed from Baltimore. This resulted from a quarrel between Hugh Auld and his brother, Thomas, who had become the legal owner of Frederick through the death of his father-in-law, Captain Anthony, and his wife, Lucretia.

Remarried to Rowena Hambleton, a woman who owned an Eastern Shore estate in Talbot County near the town of St. Michaels, Thomas Auld brought the 15-year-old Frederick there to be his slave.

Returning to rural slavery after the seven years of relative freedom he had enjoyed in Baltimore came as a great shock to Frederick. Like many adolescents, he was naturally rebellious, and now, possessed of education and religious conviction, he was proud, self-assured, and quite unfit for slavery. The young man's hatred of bondage was quickly redoubled by the rigors of plantation life. Frederick had known Thomas Auld slightly from his early years at Captain Anthony's and had a favorable impression of him largely because he was married to the boy's kindly benefactor "Miss Lucretia." But now Frederick found him a most disagreeable master and his new wife nasty and stingy. He described them as "well matched being equally mean and cruel." For the first time in seven years he suffered the pangs of hunger and was reduced to begging and stealing food. Though thievery bothered Frederick's Christian conscience, he justified it to himself by reasoning that since he was unjustly enslaved he had a legitimate right to the property of the slaveholders.

In other ways, too, Frederick showed his contempt for slavery and his new situation. He infuriated Thomas Auld by refusing to call him "Master." When sent on errands he pretended not to remember what he'd been sent for. He learned to work slowly and would often "forget" such things as tying up his master's horse or closing gates.

Still with a serious sense of having a special calling, Frederick and a pious young man named Wilson secretly opened a sabbath school to teach blacks to read the gospel. At the second meeting an angry mob, led by Thomas Auld and other leading citizens, burst in and broke up the gathering with sticks and shouts. Thus ended the school.

Soon after, Auld determined to crush young Frederick's rebellious spirit by hiring him out to Edward Covey, a local farmer with a reputation as a "slave breaker." On January 1, 1834, Frederick was placed in Covey's charge. There, for the first time in his life, he suffered the incredible hardships of harsh physical labor and the harsher whip designed to break resistance. Covey was sly and cruel. Frederick described him as "short-necked, . . . of thin and wolfish visage, with a pair of small, greenish-gray eyes." He was in the habit of sneaking up on his slaves while they worked, sometimes crawling on his hands and knees to avoid detection. Frederick and the other slaves referred to him among themselves as "the snake." Covey made their lives a living hell. He flogged Frederick so frequently that the gashes on his back remained raw and bleeding for weeks on end. These marks would be visible for the rest of Frederick's life.

Six months of such treatment left Frederick "broken in body and spirit. My natural elasticity was crushed, my intellect languished, the disposition to read departed, the cheerful spark that lingered about my eye died; the dark night of slavery closed in upon me; and behold a man transformed into a brute."

One Sunday, his only day of leisure, he stood contemplating the nearby Chesapeake Bay, "whose broad bosom was ever white with sails from every quarter of the habitable globe." Deeply affected by the white sails freely moving toward the ocean he poured out his feelings to the moving ships:

> You are loosed from your moorings, and are free; I am fast in my chains, and am a slave! You move merrily before the gentle gale, and I sadly before the bloody whip! You are freedom's swift-winged angels, that fly round the world; I am confined in bands of iron! O that I were free! O, that I were on one of your gallant decks, and under your protecting wing! . . . O God, save me! God, deliver me! Let me be free! Is there any God? Why am I a slave? I will run away. I will not stand it. . . . I have only one life to lose. I had as well be killed running as die standing. Only think of it; one hundred miles straight north, and I am free! Try it? Yes! God helping me, I will. It cannot be that I shall live and die a slave. I will take to the water. This very bay shall yet bear me into freedom.

Soon after this Frederick turned on his tormentor. He would be free or die. In an epic two-hour battle Covey finally gave way. Though Covey could have had the local constable take Frederick to the public whipping post for raising his hand against a white man, he refrained from doing so for fear his reputation as a Negro breaker would be lost. Frederick remained on the Covey farm five more months, yet never again did the "slave breaker" lift a hand against him.

This fight proved to be the turning point in Frederick's journey from slavery to freedom. As he wrote:

> It rekindled the few expiring embers of freedom, and revived within me a sense of my own manhood. It recalled the departed self-confidence, and inspired me again with a determination to be free. . . . He only can understand the deep satisfaction which I experienced, who has himself repelled by force the bloody arm of slavery. I felt as I never felt before. It was a glorious resurrection, from the tomb of slavery, to the heaven of freedom. My long-crushed spirit rose, cowardice departed, bold defiance took its place, and I now resolved that, however long I might remain a slave in form, the day had passed forever when I could be a slave in fact.

From that day forth his life was dedicated to achieving freedom—first for himself, and later for all oppressed people.

Following the fight with Covey, Frederick's life took a turn for the better. The next year Thomas Auld hired him out to another neighboring farmer, William Freeland. Here conditions were relatively good. Frederick described Mr. Freeland as "the best master I ever had, until I became my own master." Freeland gave slaves sufficient food, acted kindly, and did not overwork them. Despite this, Frederick Bailey yearned more than ever for freedom. He later explained that "if a slave has a bad master his ambition is to get one better; when he gets a better, he aspires to have the best; and when he gets the best, he aspires to be his own master."

Once again Frederick started a secret school. Meeting on Sundays as well as several evenings a week, Frederick taught not only reading, writing, and Scripture, but also discussed freedom. He would read to the group from his precious copy of *The Columbian Orator* and they would debate the "dangerous" doctrines of liberty and equality. By the end of the first year some 40 students attended Frederick's school and the young man was proud of his work. He developed ties of friendship with his fellow slaves.

Yet although treated well and able to conduct his school, this was not enough. On New Year's Day of 1836, Frederick resolved that before the year was out he would flee. He and five other slaves began seriously discussing escape, but as Frederick recalled, "whenever we suggested any plan, there was shrinking—the odds were fearful. . . . At every gate through which we were to pass, we saw a watchman—at every ferry a guard—on every bridge a sentinel—and in every wood a patrol. We were hemmed in upon every side. . . . On the one hand, there stood slavery, a stern reality, glaring frightfully upon us—its robes already crimsoned with the blood of millions, and even now feasting itself greedily upon our own flesh. On the other hand, away back in the dim distance, under the flickering light of the north star, behind some craggy hill or snow-covered mountain stood a doubtful

A sketch entitled "Negroes escaping out of slavery." The fugitives are evidently arriving in a black community, and being greeted by a crowd of sympathizers. Where possible fugitives traveled in groups composed of families and friends.

freedom—half frozen—beckoning us to come and share its hospitality."

Overcoming their fears, they resolved that even death would be preferable to remaining in hopeless bondage. They conceived a plan to steal a large canoe and on the eve of the Easter holiday paddle north up the Chesapeake. There they planned to abandon the boat and set out by foot following the North Star into the free state of Pennsylvania.

It was a bold, careful scheme and might have worked, but one of the conspirators betrayed the group. On the day they were to leave, April 2, 1836, they were rounded up, questioned in St. Michaels, and then, hitched behind horses and with their hands tied behind them, marched 12 miles to the county seat of Easton where they were put in jail.

Frederick and his co-conspirators, locked up for the crime of wanting freedom, felt the end was near. If not executed, they surely expected to be "sold down to Georgia," and indeed various slave traders milled about the jail lobby waiting their opportunity. Soon the slaves were brought before the traders and suffered the indignity of having their mouths pried open, their muscles squeezed, and their stomachs poked as though they were horses at an auction.

As it turned out, Thomas Auld could not bring himself to sell his slaves. But knowing that Frederick was their leader, and having been warned by his slaveholding father-in-law that he would shoot Frederick unless he was removed from Talbot County, Thomas Auld agreed to send the young man back to Baltimore. Perhaps realizing his slave's talents and unfitness for bondage, he promised Frederick that if he behaved himself and learned a trade, at the age of 25 he would be set free.

Frederick could scarcely believe his good fortune. Within a week he was again in the Fells Point household of Hugh and Sophia Auld. Having left in 1833 as a rebellious adolescent, he returned in 1836 a determined man. Now fully grown to over six feet, he was lean and muscular from his years of field work. He vowed to be his own man and not to bow and scrape before others simply because his skin was darker and he was considered a slave.

For the next two years he worked in the shipyards, first as an apprentice and then as a caulker, driving a rope-like fiber called oakum into a ship's planking at the seams and painting it over with boiling pitch to keep boats from leaking.

Racial prejudice proved to be a constant threat in the shipyards. Whites and blacks had built boats together for many years, but in the 1830s this was changing. Irish immigrants by the thousands crowded into Baltimore. Most were poor and had to compete for jobs with the city's more than 15,000 free blacks. Fierce racial tensions resulted. Through violence and strikes white workers succeeded in forcing many of the yards to exclude blacks. This happened at William Gardner's yard, where Frederick was first apprenticed. Ironically, he was allowed to keep his job only because he was a slave whose wages went to a white man, Hugh Auld.

The white apprentices, reflecting the rising racial hatred, did everything they could to make Frederick's life miserable. Physically he was more than a match for any of these whites and on several occasions he beat off attacks, including one by an axe-wielding apprentice. But one day four whites, armed with sticks, stones, and heavy hand spikes, managed to knock Frederick down and viciously kick him about the body. As he tried to rise he remembered that "one of their number gave me, with his heavy boot, a powerful kick in the left eye. My eyeball seemed to have burst." Witnessing this brutal attack, other white workers only encouraged Frederick's asssailants by shouting, "Kill the damned nigger! Kill him! Kill him! He struck a white person."

Barely escaping with his life, Frederick fled to his master's house. Hugh Auld was thoroughly outraged. But his effort to bring Frederick's attackers to justice was thwarted since by Maryland law no black could bring evidence against a white person. At least Auld was able to find Frederick another apprenticeship in the same yard where he worked and no further violence occurred.

By 1838 the 20-year-old Frederick had become an extremely skilled caulker whose labor could command as high a price as that of any white caulker. In May of that year he persuaded Hugh Auld to let him work on his own. It was agreed that Frederick would find his own lodging, buy his tools and clothes, and make the best working arrangements he could. His wages were to be his own, except for $3 per week that he was required to turn over to his master. Under this arrangement Frederick willingly worked harder than ever. Six days a week from sunrise to sunset he plied his trade. Now most of what he made—usually about $9 a week—was his own. He began putting away savings in what he called his "freedom fund."

Despite his long working hours, Frederick continued to find time for education, self-improvement, and socializing. In the evenings and on Sundays he associated mostly with free blacks. Sadly his boyhood white playmates, grown to manhood, had become prejudiced. These former friends who had helped to educate the slave now avoided his company. Frederick spent his most rewarding hours as a member of the East Baltimore Mental Improvement Society, a debating club where free blacks and Frederick, the sole slave, would meet to discuss topics ranging from Maryland race relations to classical mythology.

This society also organized social functions. At one of these Frederick met Anna Murray. Like him, Anna was a native of the Eastern Shore. Unlike him, however, she was free. She was drawn to the intense, intelligent bondsman. A few years older than Frederick and scarcely literate, Anna was warmhearted and practical. With her encouragement Frederick took a leading role in the debate society, sharpening his skills as a public speaker. She also inspired him to take up the violin, an instrument he delighted in playing the rest of his life. The two fell in love and in 1838 became engaged.

Marriage plans made Frederick's slavery all the more intolerable. He and Anna began plotting his escape. To help accomplish this she offered him her meager savings, accumulated from nine years' work as a housemaid. She even sold a featherbed to add to the freedom fund.

Frederick had already hit upon a scheme of escape when a dispute with Hugh Auld in the summer of 1838 caused him to put this plan into operation more quickly than he had expected. One summer weekend Frederick was a day late in giving Master Auld his $3. He had missed the payment because he was attending an all-night religious meeting and assumed his master would not mind the money being one day late. Auld, however, was furious and took away all Frederick's newly won freedoms. No longer could he live alone or keep his pay. The following week the angered slave refused to seek work and earned no money. This "strike" nearly brought the two men to blows. Though the dread of a failure exceeded what he had experienced before, Frederick once again resolved to seek his freedom.

The United States in these years was a rapidly industrializing nation. A major cause of this was the railroad. The first rail line in America, the Baltimore and Ohio, had begun commercial operations in 1830. Within a decade more than 3,000 miles of track had been laid. One line was built in 1837 between Baltimore and Wilmington, Delaware, and connected with a steamboat line for Philadelphia. Aware of this, Frederick's plan was deceptively simple. On the morning of Monday, September 3, 1838, he boarded that train just as it was pulling out of the Baltimore station. He was dressed in a sailor's suit and carried with him a "seaman's protection paper" certifying that the holder was an American sailor. Frederick had borrowed the paper from a retired merchant seaman named Stanley. The description of Stanley on the paper was of a darker and older man than Frederick, but this was the best the young man could do.

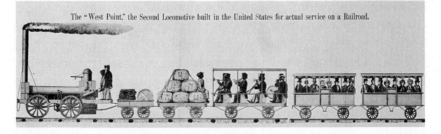

The "West Point," the Second Locomotive built in the United States for actual service on a Railroad.

The first "excursion," March 5, 1831, at Charleston, South Carolina, of the "West Point," an engine manufactured in New York City, and, as the caption says, "the second locomotive built in the United States for actual service on a railroad."

As the train began to speed at the then rapid pace of nearly 30 miles per hour through the northeastern Maryland countryside, Frederick waited nervously while the conductor made his way down the aisle. By law free blacks were required to carry freedom papers. Frederick had none; he prayed the seaman's paper would do. To fail now would surely mean jail followed by sale to the Deep South. Finally the critical moment came:

"I suppose you have your free papers?" the conductor asked.

"No sir," came Frederick's anxious reply. "I never carry my free papers to sea with me."

"But you have something to show you are a free man, have you not?"

"Yes, sir!" asserted Frederick. "I have a paper with the American eagle on it, that will carry me around the world!" With this Frederick produced the seaman's paper, which to his everlasting relief the satisfied conductor only glanced at. Frederick bought his ticket and the man moved off.

The worst seemed over. But then at Wilmington fear again gripped the runaway. Frederick's train came to a stop. Opposite it a southbound train was also halted. Frederick glanced up to see Captain McGowan for whom he had worked only days before. Tense moments followed before McGowan's train began to move. Frederick had not been recognized.

Yet no sooner had that crisis passed when Frederick spotted a man he knew seated in the same car. He was a German blacksmith named Frederick Steen. Several times Steen stared at Frederick as if he recognized him. "The heart of no fox or deer," recalled Frederick, "with hungry hounds on his trail, in full chase, could not have beaten more anxiously or noisily than did mine." However, if the blacksmith did identify him he said nothing.

Late that afternoon the former slave arrived in the free City of Brotherly Love, Philadelphia. But wishing to put more distance between himself and slavery, he inquired of a black how he could get to New York. Directed to the Willow Street depot, that evening he boarded a train for New York City. Though still scared, tired, and lonely, he was now a free man: "A new world had opened upon me. . . .

I lived more in one day than in a year of my slave life." Personal liberty achieved, Frederick was about to begin his lifelong quest for human freedom everywhere. Through great courage, nerve, and good fortune, a most extraordinary human being had emerged. Soon he would begin to speak for his whole people.

3

GARRISONIAN ABOLITIONIST

On stepping off the train in New York City on the morning of September 4, 1838, Frederick Bailey experienced a rush of excitement: "I felt like one who had escaped a den of hungry lions." This elation soon passed. Alone in America's largest city, he had no friends, no home, no food, no job, and very little money. Nor was he safe. As a fugitive he was valuable. Many New Yorkers had close connections with the slaveholding South, and professional slave catchers infested the city. By federal law, magistrates, even in the free states, were required to assist in the return of runaways. Frederick was seized by fear and loneliness. Walking amidst the throngs of people on Broadway, he dared not speak to anyone lest they turn him over to the authorities in the hope of earning a reward.

Finally in desperation he confided in a passing black sailor who directed him to the home of David Ruggles. This was an excellent choice. Ruggles was secretary of the New York Vigilance Committee and publisher of *The Mirror of Liberty*, an antislavery quarterly and the first magazine put out by a black. He also was part of the underground railroad—an informal network of abolitionists and sympathizers who provided legal, financial, and human assistance to fugitive slaves. Safely hidden in Ruggles's house, Frederick wrote to Anna Murray, who soon joined him. On September 15 they were married.

Knowing New York to be unsafe, Ruggles suggested that the young couple resettle in New Bedford, Massachusetts, a community where antislavery sentiment was more prevalent and slave catchers rare. New Bedford was also a bustling whaling port with a number of active shipyards. Ruggles assumed that Frederick could find work there as a caulker.

Frederick and Anna followed Ruggles's advice. Two days after their wedding they arrived in New Bedford at the home of Mr. and Mrs. Nathan Johnson, friends of Ruggles. This generous black couple quickly made the newlyweds part of their family. Nathan Johnson also suggested the surname of "Douglass" for the escaped slave, since going by his real name was too dangerous. Having recently read Sir Walter Scott's *Lady of the Lake*, Johnson was impressed by the heroic Scottish lord of that name. And so Frederick Augustus Washington Bailey became Frederick Douglass, a name that within less than a decade would become renowned on two continents.

Soon after their arrival Frederick Douglass found his first employment as a free man, loading oil on a sloop bound for New York. Though it was dirty, back-breaking work, he performed it gladly: "I was now my own master. It was a happy moment, the rapture of which can be understood only by those who have been slaves. It was the first work, the reward of which was to be entirely my own. . . . I was at work for myself and newly-married wife. It was to me the starting-point of a new existence."

The next day when Douglass sought work as a caulker, he learned a bitter lesson: racial prejudice was not confined to the South. The white caulkers of New Bedford refused to work with blacks. Dismayed, Douglass was forced to take various odd jobs as a common laborer. For the next three years he was employed at such tasks as sawing wood, shoveling coal, sweeping chimneys, driving a coach, and operating the bellows of a factory furnace. Such hard, menial jobs paid about $1 per day, only half of what he would have received had prejudice not closed the caulking profession to him.

His wife, Anna, helped greatly during these years of struggle. In addition to making their small apartment comfortable and homelike, she supplemented their meager earnings by taking in washing and doing domestic work. In June 1839 Rosetta, their first child, was born. Late in 1840 Anna bore a son, Lewis. Though poor, they were a free and happy family.

Despite the long hours of hard work, Douglass continued his religious and intellectual development. Finding that blacks were treated as second-class citizens in the white Methodist church of New Bedford, he joined the Zion Methodists. In this black congregation he soon became a class leader and occasional preacher. He also began attending various local meetings of the black community, where he further developed his skills in public debate.

One day some four months after his arrival in New Bedford, a copy of William Lloyd Garrison's newspaper, the *Liberator*, came into his hands. Reading this was a revelation to Douglass. Though he had hated slavery nearly his entire life and possessed some knowledge of the antislavery movement, he had not fully thought out its principles. Now in the pages of the *Liberator* he found the evils of slavery unsparingly denounced and the doctrine of immediate emancipation lucidly argued as an absolute moral and Christian duty.

Garrison's agitation against slavery had begun in 1829 when at age 24 he had become coeditor of Benjamin Lundy's *The Genius of Universal Emancipation*. This paper was published in Baltimore with offices scarcely a mile from the Auld house where the young Frederick served as a slave. At that time neither Garrison nor Douglass was aware of the other's existence, and in little more than a year Garrison fled Baltimore after having been imprisoned because of his scathing editorials against the domestic slave trade.

Back in his native New England, Garrison determined to launch his own antislavery paper. Begun in Boston on January 1, 1831, Garrison's *Liberator* struck a new note of militancy in the hitherto moderate white antislavery movement. Previous to Garrison most antislavery advocates believed that blacks could never live as the equals of whites in America. Their idea for ending slavery was to gradually persuade slaveholders to free their slaves and to then transport these freed slaves back to Africa. To Garrison, colonization was a fraud. He believed that blacks were American citizens and must be granted all civil rights in this country.

In place of colonization Garrison offered a simple, radical plan: the immediate abolition of all slavery. In the first issue of the *Liberator* he wrote, "I determined at every hazard, to lift up the standard of emancipation in the eyes of the nation, within sight of Bunker Hill and in the birth place of liberty. That standard is now unfurled; and long may it float, unhurt by the spoilations of time or the missiles of a desperate foe—yea, till every chain be broken, and every bondman set free! Let the Southern oppressors tremble—let their Northern apologists tremble—let all the enemies of the persecuted blacks tremble."

In issue after issue, Garrison attacked slavery as a sin and a violation of basic American principles embodied in the Declaration of Independence. To Garrison, slavery was an absolute evil that could only be ended by immediate and unconditional abolition. Since the organized churches and the state were not completely opposed to slavery, he considered these institutions immoral.

Not content to merely write condemnations of slavery, in 1832 Garrison helped found the New England Anti-Slavery Society. The following year he drafted the Declaration of Principles for the American Anti-Slavery Society. Soon a small but dedicated group of men and women, blacks and whites, flocked to the cause. Motivated by Christian ethics and the ideals of American democracy, they spoke out strongly and clearly against slavery because, as Douglass's benefactor David Ruggles put it, "the pleas of crying soft and sparing never answered the purpose of reform and never will." Garrisonians hoped to convert America to their cause by a mass propaganda campaign, or what they termed "moral suasion."

This new antislavery movement was part of a general upsurge of reform activity in the 1830s and 1840s. Religious revivals gave rise to widespread belief in human perfectability.

All manner of moral wrongs and social injustices were targeted for elimination. People united in various organizations advocating everything from opposition to alcoholic beverages (the temperance movement), to prison reform, women's rights, and world peace. It was the greatest upsurge of reform activity in American history, and no movement was more important than abolitionism.

Beginning with only a few hundred members in the early 1830s, antislavery organizations grew quickly. By 1838, the year of Douglass's escape, there were more than 600 abolitionist societies in Massachusetts, New York, and Ohio alone. By 1841 when Douglass first heard Garrison, more than 2,000 societies existed with collective membership of over 200,000.

Immediately after first reading a copy of Garrison's paper, Douglass subscribed to it. Every week he read and reread it, quickly mastering Garrisonian principles and philosophy. "The paper became my meat and my drink," he later wrote. "My soul was set all on fire. Its sympathy for my bretheren in bonds—its scathing denuciations of slaveholders—its faithful exposures of slavery—and its powerful attacks upon the upholders of the institution—sent a thrill of joy through my soul, such as I had never felt before!"

Douglass's conversion to Garrisonianism was akin to a religious experience. Like the earlier fight with Covey, it caused a rebirth of his sense of mission. In his words it "was literally the opening upon me of a new heaven and a new earth—the whole world had for me a new face and life itself a new meaning. I saw myself a new man, and a new and happy future for my downtrodden and enslaved fellow countrymen."

Flushed with this enthusiasm, Douglass began playing an important role in New Bedford abolitionist activities. As early as March 1839, a speech of his condemning schemes to colonize blacks in Africa was mentioned in the *Liberator*. In June 1841 he chaired a meeting called to oppose plans to remove free blacks forcibly from the state of Maryland. On August 9, 1841, Douglass attended the annual meeting of the

Bristol County Anti-Slavery Society, held that year in New Bedford. William Lloyd Garrison was present. Having learned to admire Garrison through his paper, Douglass was naturally predisposed to love the man. He was not disappointed. To Douglass the soft-spoken Garrison was "calm and serene as a summer sky, and as pure." He was "the Moses, raised up by God, to deliver his modern Israel from bondage."

Elated at his initial encounter with Garrison, the following day, August 10, 1841, Douglass took his first time off from work to accompany the *Liberator* editor and some 40 others who were leaving to attend an antislavery convention on the island of Nantucket. When the convention opened the next morning, Douglass, to his astonishment, was called upon to speak. Though accustomed to addressing black audiences, the idea of speaking before Mr. Garrison and other whites made him extremely nervous. Trembling and embarrassed he got up and spoke about his life as a slave. Despite his nervousness, the speech was a great success. "Flinty hearts were pierced," wrote one reporter, "and cold ones melted by his eloquence." Deeply moved, Garrison followed with an address based upon Douglass's remarks.

Before the convention adjourned, John A. Collins, general agent of the Massachusetts Anti-Slavery Society urged Douglass to become a full-time lecturer for that organization. Still unsure of his abilities, Douglass was reluctant to accept, though after much pleading from Garrison and others he agreed to a three-month appointment. He would remain in this position for four years. For the 23-year-old fugitive, just three years removed from slavery, a great career was about to begin. Douglass would play many roles in his life, but none more significant than as a lecturer.

Soon in company with such well-known abolitionists as Garrison, Collins, Wendell Phillips, James Buffum, Abby Kelley, Charles Remond, Parker Pillsbury, and Stephen Foster, Douglass was criss-crossing New England, New York State, and the Ohio Valley in the cause of freedom. Typically, abolitionist speakers traveled in pairs and might make two or three addresses a day for weeks on end. For Douglass this meant long absences from home and family. But he earned more than he had as a common laborer and the lecture circuit served to further his education and increase his maturity. From the outset his speeches were enthusiastically received.

Douglass could not have entered the services of the antislavery movement at a better moment. Though abolitionists like Garrison had been speaking about the injustice and immorality of slavery, they were Northern whites whose testimony could easily be dismissed as exaggeration not based on firsthand experience. For many years Southern apologists had been painting a very rosy picture of slavery and had been able to convince a great many Northerners that what they said was true. Slavery, they argued, was divinely sanctioned and beneficial to the Negro. Blacks, it was claimed, were well fed, well housed, well clothed, and well cared for from birth to death. They were a simple people and happy with their lot. Much proslavery literature contrasted the contented life of the slave with the miserable conditions suffered by free workers in the North.

In Douglass, the abolitionists had the solid evidence they needed to refute such proslavery arguments. Here was a man who had lived for 20 years in bondage and whose whip-scarred back was visible proof of slavery's brutality. Here was a man who had risked everything to escape. Here was a man whose strength of character, intelligence, and independence destroyed the Southern argument that blacks were naturally inferior, childlike, and happy with the paternal care of slavery. Here was no mere copy of other antislavery speakers, but a true representative of black America who had known pain and prejudice throughout his life. Douglass's story delivered from the lecture platform revealed in concrete terms just how abominable slavery really was.

In his early lectures Douglass had to be careful not to say too much about himself lest he risk recapture. He became adept at describing particulars while at the same time leaving out names and places. So adroit was Douglass at this that he fooled one North Carolina editor into announcing that "this Frederick is a runaway negro, the property of Governor Dudley, of this state."

Douglass's speeches were powerful indictments of the slavery system. He would declare to audiences that "he stood before them that night as a thief and a robber! This head, these limbs, this body, I have stolen from my *master!*" On another occasion he told his listeners: "Yes, my blood has sprung out as the lash embedded itself in my flesh. And yet my master has the reputation of being a pious man and a good Christian. He was a class leader in the Methodist church. I have seen this pious class leader cross and tie the hands of one of his young female slaves, and lash her on the bare skin and justify the deed by the quotation from the Bible, 'he who knoweth his master's will and doeth it not, shall be beaten with many stripes.'" Such descriptions had great impact on audiences. Many unsympathetic to the abolitionist cause were converted after listening to Douglass.

Very quickly this new employee of the Massachusetts Anti-Slavery Society became one of the greatest attractions among abolitionist speakers. "He is very fluent in the use of language," wrote the editor of *The Hingham Patriot*, "choice and appropriate language, too; and talks as well, for all we could see, as men who have spent all their lives over books. He is forcible, keen and very sarcastic; and considering the poor advantages he must have had as a slave, he is certainly a remarkable man."

Listening to lectures was a favorite nineteenth-century pastime. In this age before radio and television, people thought nothing of sitting on hard benches, standing in crowded halls, or in the open air for hours on end to hear speakers. Oratory served the purposes of politics, reform, religion, education, and entertainment. Many of the best-known people of the era were famous lecturers. There were politicians such as Daniel Webster and Henry Clay; reformers such as Dorothea Dix and Horace Mann; religious leaders such as William Ellery Channing and Charles Grandison Finney; intellectuals such as Ralph Waldo Emerson and

Margaret Fuller; abolitionists such as Wendell Phillips and Sojourner Truth. But by the mid-forties, Frederick Douglass took second place to no one when it came to delivering a speech.

The sources of Douglass's oratorical skills were many and varied. As a young slave on the vast Lloyd plantation he had listened to the stories told by older blacks. This oral tradition was a rich part of Afro-American culture and good storytellers were highly revered on the plantation. Douglass also had heard many revivalist preachers, black and white, and had himself begun preaching at an early age. His participation in debating societies in both Baltimore and New Bedford also helped to hone his skills. In addition he read many great speeches as well as novels by Dickens, Scott, Alexandre Dumas, and various other authors. The Bible, too, was an inspiration, particularly the Sermon on the Mount.

But perhaps the greatest influence on Douglass's oratory was the first book he ever bought, *The Columbian Orator*. Not only did this volume contain examples of excellent speeches, but also an essay "General Directions for Speaking." This piece by Caleb Bingham had been written in the late eighteenth century, before the rise of the more flowery romantic styles that predominated in Douglass's day. It recommended a direct, clear style. "It is the orator's business . . . to follow nature, and to endeavor that the tone of his voice appear natural and unaffected." Bingham also emphasized varying the tone of voice and using different gestures and expressions.

Douglass became a master of Bingham's techniques. While typical nineteenth-century speeches were filled with classical allusions, Latin phrases, and overly rich imagery, his were refreshingly straightforward. As one reporter noted, Douglass's "language is classically chaste, not groaning under the flowery ornaments of school boy declamation, but terse yet eloquent, like a piece of finished sculpture beautiful in every outline of symmetrical and unadorned simplicity."

Douglass also captivated audiences by his appearance, voice, and expressions. Over six feet tall in an age of relatively short men and women, his was a commanding presence on the platform. Broad shouldered and physically attractive, he was described variously as "bold," "manly," "striking," "imposing," and "majestic." Swedish visitor Frederika Bremer portrayed him as having "an unusually handsome exterior, such as I imagine should belong to an Arab chief. Those beautiful eyes were full of dark fire."

Possessed of a deep, melodious voice, he could by turns be humble, sincere, humorous, sarcastic, and indignant. Generally opening his lectures speaking slowly and almost quietly, Douglass's voice would increase in intensity and volume. "His voice is full and rich," observed an Ohio reporter, "and his enunciation remarkably distinct and musical. He speaks in a low conversational tone most of the time, but occasionally his tones roll out full and deep as those of an organ. The effect is electrical."

Not only did Douglass have the voice of a great actor, but other theatrical skills as well. He could perform comic or tragic scenes, and as a mimic he was unsurpassed. A particular favorite with audiences was his imitation of the Southern white minister exhorting the slaves to obey their masters: "You cannot appreciate your blessings; you know not how happy a thing it is for you, that you were born of that portion of the human family which has the working, instead of the thinking, to do! Oh! how grateful and obedient you ought to be to your masters!" He also satirized through mimicry such public figures as Webster, Clay, and John C. Calhoun. Through such expressive mockery as well as jokes and anecdotes Douglass maintained a light touch that audiences loved. But he was able to do this without losing sight of the crucial issues under consideration.

Douglass had great impact on nearly everyone who heard him. A long-time abolitionist in a letter to Garrison wrote: "It has been my fortune to hear a great many anti-slavery lecturers, and many distinguished speakers on other subjects; but it has rarely been my lot to listen to one whose power over me was greater than Douglass, and not over *me* only, but over all who heard him." Black abolitionist William Wells Brown, who often appeared on the speaker's platform with Douglass, expressed a similar sentiment: "White men and black men had talked against slavery, but none had ever spoken like Frederick Douglass." To a Detroit reporter he was simply "the greatest orator of modern times."

Despite Douglass's popularity, being an abolitionist in the 1840s was not all applause and fame. Southern slaveholders, of course, hated the abolitionists. But so, too, did many Northerners. Some of this resentment came from Northern business interests with close ties to the South. Many workers feared that if the slaves were freed they would come North and take jobs from whites. Other Northerners viewed abolitionism as a dangerous threat to the social order. Politicians resented the antislavery movement for stirring up an issue that threatened to disrupt the national political parties. But the major cause of anti-abolitionist feeling in the North was racial prejudice. Few whites could conceive of a society in which the two races would live together on equal terms. Intermarriage between the races was especially dreaded.

The rise of the radical Garrisonians in the 1830s had been met by an eruption of anti-abolitionist riots often led by the most respected citizens. Numerous antislavery meetings were forcibly broken up. In New York City the home of abolitionist Lewis Tappan was burned. In southern Illinois abolitionist newspaper publisher Elijah P. Lovejoy was killed while defending his press from an angry mob. Even in Massachusetts, where antislavery sentiment was most widespread, Garrison was nearly killed by an angry lynch mob who dragged him through the streets of Boston with a rope about his neck.

By the time Frederick Douglass joined the abolitionist lecture circuit, mob violence had subsided somewhat, but was still a serious problem. At almost all his speaking engagements hecklers were present. Often eggs and overripe fruits were thrown. On September 15, 1843, in Pendleton, Indiana, Douglass was severely beaten and was lucky to escape with only bruises and a broken wrist.

This scene depicts rioters at Alton, Illinois, setting fire to a warehouse containing the printing press of an antislavery minister, Elijah Lovejoy. Rev. Lovejoy lost his life defending the warehouse from the mob, November 7, 1837

Being an abolitionist under such circumstances took great courage. But being a black abolitionist was twice as dangerous. Racists regularly singled out Douglass for attack. Even such things as traveling to and from meetings and dining and sleeping at hotels subjected black abolitionists to humiliating discrimination. Wherever Douglass went he encountered prejudice. Stage drivers, steamboat captains, railroad conductors, and innkeepers routinely attempted to segregate him from whites. Douglass always tried to combat such segregation. If refused service at a restaurant he would politely ask why. When no satisfactory explanation was given he would remain seated even if this led to his removal by force. On one occasion he held so tightly to an Eastern Railway seat from which six railroad employees were ejecting him that he tore the seat and several others from the train floor. To Douglass segregation was merely an extension of slavery, an attempt to deprive him of his hard-won freedom.

But hostile crowds and discriminatory policies were not the only difficulties Douglass experienced as an abolitionist lecturer. Gradually he came to question the role expected of him by Garrison and other movement leaders. From the outset he was treated somewhat patronizingly as a "prize exhibit": a fugitive who could testify to the evils of slavery from firsthand experience. "Give us the facts," John Collins told him, "we will take care of the philosophy." Collins would introduce Douglass as a recent "graduate from the 'peculiar institution' with his diploma written on his back." Douglass would then get up and tell his story. Collins even worried that the ex-slave's clear diction ought to be disguised in the interest of "authenticity." "Better to have a little of the plantation speech than not," he was advised; "it is not best that you seem too learned."

Douglass grew restive under these instructions. As he gained greater confidence in his speaking skills his keen intellect led him to expand the focus of his talks. Though he still frequently told about the horrors of slavery drawn from personal experience, his speeches became more wide-ranging and analytical. He discussed the proslavery character of the churches, the nature of the Constitution, Northern racial prejudice, black suffrage, the imprisonment of fugitive slaves, and many other issues.

To their credit Garrison and other white abolitionists did not discourage Douglass from taking on these larger subjects. Soon Douglass's oratorical skill combined with his brilliant analyses moved him to the forefront of abolitionist lecturers. Yet the more polished he became the more audiences questioned his authenticity. Surely, people thought, such a cultivated, intelligent individual could not be but a few years removed from the brutal slave system. Why, people asked, if he was a slave was he so vague about where he had lived, who his master had been, how he had escaped?

Bothered by such questions, in the fall of 1844, Frederick Douglass decided to throw caution to the wind. He would write a book and reveal all: who he was, who's slave he had been, how he had suffered and plotted, his education, the fight with Covey, his escape—everything. Though knowing that such a book might lead to his recapture and return to bondage,

Douglass sat down during the winter and early spring of 1844-1845 and wrote the story of his life. This book would prove to be a major force in the antislavery movement as well as a classic of American autobiography. It also initiated a new phase of his remarkable career.

4

A BOOK AND A JOURNEY

On April 22, 1845, soon after reading the manuscript of Douglass's autobiography, Wendell Phillips wrote the author:

> My Dear Friend:
> You remember the old fable of "The Man and the Lion," where the lion complained that he should not be so misrepresented "when the lions wrote history."
> I am glad the time has come when the "lions write history."

A "lion" indeed had written history—his own and that of slavery personally experienced. Published in May of that year as the *Narrative of the Life of Frederick Douglass an American Slave*, this book quickly became a great success. Within three years more than 11,000 copies had been sold in the United States—a large sale for that time. When issued in England, it rapidly went through nine editions. German and French translations also sold well.

Praise for Douglass's writing was profuse. Margaret Fuller, the noted feminist, reviewing the *Narrative* in the *New York Tribune*, had this to say: "Considered merely as a narrative, we never read one more simple, true, coherent and warm with genuine feeling. It is an excellent piece of writing, and on that score to be prized as a specimen of the powers of the black race, which prejudice persists in disputing." Another reviewer proclaimed the *Narrative* "the most thrilling work which the American press ever issued—*and the most important. If it does not open the eyes of this people, they must be petrified into eternal sleep.*"

Douglass's account of his life in bondage was not the first of its kind. By the mid-1840s slave narratives had become commonplace. By the time of the Civil War some 80 such autobiographies had been published. These accounts not only appealed to abolitionists, but also to Northern readers intrigued by dramas of escape or interested in the unique world of the South.

Of all the slave autobiographies, none had more literary merit, authenticity, or influence than Douglass's *Narrative*. Like all great autobiography, his story was the creation of a particularly perceptive person. In straightforward, often vivid prose, Douglass described the multifaceted slave experience: life on the plantation, the small farm, and in the city; good masters and bad; various types of slaves and free blacks. The book revealed the horrors of slavery without resorting to exaggeration or melodrama. Douglass's story had a message: the evil of slavery was the ownership of human beings. Whether bound to a cruel Covey or a lenient Freeland was not the point—freedom was. To be less than free was to be less than human. This indictment moved countless readers to condemn the oppressive slave system.

Yet while Douglass's *Narrative* served the abolitionist cause, it threatened to end the author's career as an antislavery advocate. No longer would people doubt Douglass's authenticity, but in being so specific he had jeopardized his liberty. Abolitionist friends suggested a trip to Great Britain. There he would be safe from recapture and at the same time could help further the cause. In 1833 slavery had been abolished in the British empire after years of antislavery agitation. Many of the men and women who had worked in Britain's abolitionist movement had also shown concern for the plight of the American slave. It was now hoped that Douglass, in the words of one of his abolitionist friends, would excite "a deeper hatred in the breasts of English people of American slavery. . . . When they shall see before them a man so noble and eloquent as Frederick, and learn from his own lips, that he is only seven years out of bondage; that he has now the marks of the whip upon his back, which he will carry with him until the day of his death, that he has near and dear relatives that are now pining in bondage; they will realize to a considerable extent, the horrors of the American slave trade; the effect cannot be otherwise than good."

The idea of the trip excited Douglass. He would "seek a refuge from republican slavery in monarchical England." Naturally he was reluctant to be separated from Anna and his children, but he and his wife agreed it would be for the best. Three years earlier in 1842 the family had moved from New Bedford to Lynn, Massachusetts. That year a second son, Frederick, Jr., was born. In 1844 Anna bore a third son, whom they named Charles Remond after a friend and fellow black abolitionist. To support the family in his absence Frederick arranged that Anna and the children would receive the proceeds from the sale of the *Narrative*.

On August 16, 1845, Douglass embarked on the Cunard sail-steamship *Cambria*. He was accompanied by James Buffum, a Lynn neighbor and close abolitionist associate, and the four Hutchinsons, a celebrated antislavery singing group. But unfortunately the British-owned Cunard Line did not wish to offend white America. Consequently Douglass's request to book a first-class cabin was denied. He was given a berth in the steerage compartment below the waterline where cargo and cattle were stored. In spite of this and seasickness, Douglass enjoyed the trip. He was allowed to be with his friends during the day on the promenade deck, and many passengers befriended him.

While on board the *Cambria*, Douglass had an encounter with slaveholders. "I was very well known to the passengers," he told audiences soon after landing in Britain, "and there was quite a curiosity to hear me speak on the subject of slavery." When the captain invited him to give an address, Douglass agreed. But as soon as he began to speak, he "observed a determination on the part of some half a dozen to prevent my speaking, who I found were slave owners. I had not uttered more than a sentence than up started a man from Connecticut, and said, 'that's a lie!'"

Pandemonium broke out. "Down with the nigger," said one, and "he shan't speak," said another. Douglass sat quietly with his arms folded. "I never saw a more barefaced attempt," he said, "to put down the freedom of speech than upon this occasion." The captain now intervened, and attempted to restore order after knocking down one slaveowner with his fist. "I have done all I could," the captain said when quiet was restored,

> to make the voyage agreeable to all. We have had a little of everything on board. We have had all sorts of discussions, . . . we have had singing and dancing, everything that we could have, except an anti-slavery speech, and since there were a number of ladies and gentlemen interested in Mr. Douglass, I requested him to speak. Now, those who are not desirous to hear him, let them go to another part of the vessel.

The slaveowners quieted down and stopped making threats when the captain told them that he would put them in irons if they did not. But the attempt to silence Douglass had the opposite effect. "The agitation did not cease," said Douglass, "for the question was discussed, to the moment we landed in Liverpool."

Furious at having been humiliated on account of a black, the slaveholders upon landing at Liverpool the next day told their story to the British press. But this backfired. The British papers sided with Douglass, and almost overnight he became the center of national interest with a ready audience.

After a brief stay in Liverpool, Douglass and Buffum parted from the Hutchinsons and sailed for Ireland. Arriving in Dublin, they stayed with Richard Webb, an antislavery advocate and printer. Webb was a cordial host and helped arrange a number of antislavery rallies for the Americans. He also printed an edition of the *Narrative* that sold well wherever Douglass spoke. From the outset Douglass was a sensation. Within a few weeks of his arrival in Dublin he wrote excitedly to Garrison that "our success here is even greater than I had anticipated. We have held four glorious anti-slavery meetings—two in Royal Exchange, and two in the Friends' meeting-house—all crowded to overflowing."

Irish enthusiasm for the 27-year-old ex-slave knew no bounds. To audiences he was a romantic hero. They loved his eloquence, his wit, his manly bearing. Newspaper accounts variously described his audiences as "most numerous and respectable," "crowded to excess," "unexpectedly large," and "densely crowded." Listeners seemed to find in Douglass not just the champion of the slave but the defender of all downtrodden peoples, including themselves. Ireland at the time of Douglass's arrival was experiencing the beginnings of a potato blight that would last for several years. Desperate poverty and starvation were widespread. In addition the predominantly Catholic Irish even suffered from religious persecution at the hands of their British rulers. Absentee landlordism and overpopulation were also serious problems.

The warm receptions and huge audiences greatly pleased Douglass. He quickly came to love Ireland and remained there nearly five months. From Dublin he traveled to Cork and later on to Belfast. Everywhere he went he was treated as a celebrity. He was introduced by mayors; he was dined and entertained by members of Parliament; he exchanged pleasantries with nobles. Early on during his Dublin visit Douglass attended a lecture by the aged Daniel O'Connell, the leader of the Irish emancipation movement and one of the great reformers of the age. Hearing this man, whose printed speech in *The Columbian Orator* had so moved him as a young slave, was a thrill for Douglass.

Though most of Douglass's public appearances were devoted to denouncing slavery, from the outset of his travels he also became involved in a variety of other reforms. He was particularly active in the temperance crusade. He gave a number of temperance lectures and even signed a pledge to abstain from alcohol. Additionally, he publicly supported free trade, home rule for Ireland, and extension of the suffrage. As he explained in a letter to Garrison: "though I am more closely connected and identified with one class of outraged, oppressed and enslaved people, I cannot allow myself to be insensible to the wrongs and sufferings of any part of the great family of man. I am not only an American slave, but a man, and as such, am bound to use my powers for the welfare of the whole human brotherhood." Taking up causes not directly his own was a liberating experience for Douglass. his quest for freedom had broadened. *"All great reforms go together,"* he proclaimed in an address before the Cork Temperance Institute. "Whatever tends to exalt humanity in one portion of the world, tends to exalt it in another part."

These months in Ireland were among the happiest in Douglass's life. It was not due just to the crowds who adored him or the notables who feted him. Above all it resulted from the complete lack of racial prejudice he experienced. Here he could eat at restaurants, sleep in hotels, visit theaters and museums without fear of rejection. He was accepted as a person. Even being seen in the company of white women evoked no hostile comments.

Reflecting on these enjoyable months on the eve of his departure from Ireland, Douglass wrote to Garrison: "I seem to have undergone a transformation. I live a new life. . . . In the Southern part of the United States I was a slave, thought of and spoken of as property . . . *a chattel in the hands of my owners* . . . . In the Northern states, a fugitive slave, liable to be hunted at any moment like a felon, . . . denied the privileges and courtesies common to others in the use of the most humble means of conveyance—shut out from the cabins on steamboats—refused admission to respectable hotels—caricatured, scorned, scoffed, mocked." In Ireland all this changed: "I breathe, and lo the chattel becomes a man. . . . I employ a cab—I am seated beside white people—I reach the hotel—I enter the same door—I am shown into the same parlor—I dine at the same table—and no one is offended. No delicate nose grows deformed in my presence. . . . I am met by no upturned nose and scornful lip to tell me, '*We don't allow niggers in here!*'" No wonder, then, that these first European experiences were so important to Douglass. Throughout his nearly two-year stay in the British Isles he never was treated as inferior simply because of his skin color.

From Ireland Douglass moved on to Scotland, arriving in Glasgow with Buffum in late January of 1846. Here, too, he attracted great attention. At the time of his arrival a controversy was raging about the Free Church of Scotland. Having broken with the Established Presbyterian Church of Scotland in 1843 over the right of individual congregations to choose their own ministers, the Free Church had launched a fundraising campaign. Southern slaveholding Presbyterians, most of whose ancestors had been Scottish, contributed heavily to the Free Church. British abolitionists, however, questioned the propriety of accepting the "blood-stained" dollars of slaveholders. A vigorous campaign was launched to pressure the Free Church to return the money.

Douglass and Buffum threw themselves wholeheartedly into this new cause. Though repudiated by Free Church conservatives as "strangers unknown to respectable people in the country," the Americans drew huge and excited crowds wherever they lectured. Speaking in halls and churches decorated with banners proclaiming, "SEND BACK THE MONEY," Douglass maintained "that man-stealing is incompatible with Christianity; that slaveholding and true religion are at war with each other; and that a Free Church should have no fellowship with a slave church." According to a Glasgow paper Douglass's speeches "rivetted the attention of his numerous [audiences] every night." Another paper reported that Douglass's "surprising natural eloquence" caused the "most unequivocal expressions" of audience support. Scotland, yet another newsman claimed, had been thrown into "a blaze of anti-slavery agitation."

By the spring of 1846 the "Send Back the Money" campaign was at its height. "Frederick Douglass," wrote abolitionist Mary Welsh, had "done wonders in opening the eyes of the public to this enormous iniquity, never was there such excitement created as at present." A typical meeting took place on 1 May 1846 at the Music Hall in Edinburgh. Though admission was charged, more than 2,000 people filled the hall to overflowing. Joining Douglass on the platform were his friend Buffum, Henry C. Wright, another Garrisonian abolitionist, and George Thompson, one of the best-known British antislavery advocates and Douglass's and Buffum's host in Edinburgh. Douglass told the cheering audience that when the Free Church "members become fully alive to the odium and disgrace they are incurring for the sake of clutching the stained hand of the man-stealer—then shall the money be sent back."

Ultimately the "Send Back the Money" crusade failed. Free Church leaders refused to give in to popular agitation. Nevertheless, this campaign did have several positive results. First, it rekindled antislavery sentiment throughout the British Isles. Second, it dramatized the connection between American slavery and British behavior. Finally, it made the name of Frederick Douglass famous and assured that the American fugitive would continue to draw large and enthusiastic audiences.

In early May of 1846 Douglass left Scotland and traveled overland to England. He appeared in London for the first time on May 18 to address the annual convention of the British and Foreign Anti-Slavery Society. Though this organization was anti-Garrisonian, Douglass considered it his duty to "speak in any meeting where freedom of speech is allowed and where I may do anything toward exposing the bloody system of slavery." These Londoners for their part, never having seen Douglass, were eager to hear the man who would, according to William Sharman Crawford, detail "the miseries to which the American slaves are subjected: and vindicate the talents and abilities of the African people." The audience was not disappointed. Douglass's "long and eloquent speech" was the high point of the convention.

So eager were London reformers to hear Douglass that he received requests to address meetings of peace, suffrage, and temperance groups in addition to the antislavery convention. Then on May 22, he was the guest of honor at an antislavery rally in which nearly 3,000 people crowded London's Finsbury Chapel almost "to suffocation." "Let the slaveholders of America know," he said, "that the curtain which conceals their crimes is being lifted abroad; that we are opening the dark cell, and leading the people into the dark recesses of what they are pleased to call their domestic institution. We want them to know that a knowledge of their whippings, their scourgings, their brandings, their chainings, is not confined to their plantations, but that some negro of theirs has broken loose from his chains . . . and is now exposing their deeds to the gaze of the Christian people of England" [immense cheers]. "I expose slavery," he went on, "because to expose it is to kill it. . . . I want the slaveholder surrounded by a wall of antislavery fire, ..."

At Finsbury Chapel Frederick Douglass spoke for three hours. Never before, claimed British abolitionist John Campbell, had the audience heard a slave with "so much logic—so much wit—so much fancy—so much eloquence." In a letter to Garrison, Douglass described that gathering as "one of the most effective and satisfactory meetings which I have attended since landing on these shores."

In late June of that year Douglass saw Buffum and the Hutchinsons off from Liverpool. Though on his own, Douglass by now had numerous British friends and a full schedule of speaking engagements. He also looked forward to the arrival of his friend and mentor, William Lloyd Garrison.

On July 31, 1846 Garrison landed at Liverpool. Douglass who had again been lecturing in Scotland, hurried to join him. Early August found the two abolitionists traveling to London to attend the World Temperance Convention. Though not an official delegate, Douglass was asked to speak. Coming to the podium after a number of uncritical speeches on the progress of temperance in America and Britain, Douglass threw the convention into an uproar. He began by relating how slaveholders used alcohol to weaken the slaves' natural aspirations for liberty. He then launched into an attack on the American temperance movement for failing to address the problem of drink in the slave system. Some 3 million slaves stood outside the reach of the American Temperance Society. Douglass further faulted the American movement for its in-

William Lloyd Garrison, Douglass's first antislavery mentor, who joined him in lecture tours both in the United States and in England.

difference and even hostility to the temperance efforts of Northern free blacks. He noted the experience of Philadelphia blacks whose efforts to organize a temperance society had led to their being assaulted by an angry white mob; their members had been beaten and their temperance hall and church destroyed. Before he could continue in this vein, Douglass was cut short by the irate chairman. Amidst cries of "Go on! Go on!" as well as some hisses, he sat down.

American delegates were furious. In an angry rebuttal published in the *New York Evangelist*, the Reverend Samuel H. Cox, a temperance advocate and professed abolitionist, accused Douglass of being an extremist who perversely "lugged in antislavery" to disrupt the grand cause of temperance. What right had a black man to speak "as if he had been our schoolmaster, and we his docile and devoted pupils?" Cox even implied that Douglass was in the pay of extremists trying to ridicule America before an international audience.

Douglass responded with a letter to the *Liberator*. Cox, he suggested, was mainly upset that a black had stood upon the platform "on terms of perfect equality with a pure white American gentleman!" Until the barriers of slavery and racial prejudice were broken, he argued, temperance would not be effective among America's millions of blacks. As for Cox's alleged abolitionist sympathies, Douglass wrote: "Who ever heard of a true abolitionist speaking of slavery as an 'imputed evil,' or complain of being 'wounded and injured' by an allusion to it—and that, too, because the allusion was in opposition to the infernal system?" To Douglass, Cox's pretensions of being an abolitionist were either "brazen hyprocrisy or self-deception."

Such an episode might not have occurred before Douglass's trip abroad. Traveling outside his racially biased native land had made him bolder. Not only did he speak out on more subjects, he also spoke more forcefully. In Europe people listened to him and respected him as a man, at home he was a mere chattel. Living abroad compelled Douglass to confront his mixed feelings about the United States. "In thinking of America," he had written in an earlier letter sent to Garrison from Ireland, "I sometimes find myself admiring her bright blue sky, her grand old woods, her fertile fields, her beautiful rivers, her mighty lakes, and star crowned mountains." But this reverie was cut short by his recognition that America "welcomes me to her shores only as a slave. . . . I am an outcast from the society of my childhood, and an outlaw in the land of my birth." Such reflections forced the fugitive slave to conclude that "if ever I had any patriotism, or any capacity for the feeling, it was whipped out of me long since, by the lash of American soul-drivers."

These feelings made Douglass less willing to tolerate the hypocrisy of "artful dodgers" like Cox. Throughout his stay in the British Isles he took every opportunity to point out that the sin of slavery did not rest with the Southern slaveholder alone. Even well meaning groups like the American Temperance Society, by their unwillingness to take up the cause of black Americans, shared in the guilt of slavery, just as did the pious Free Church people in Scotland.

Following the London temperance meeting, Douglass and Garrison spent much of the summer and fall of 1846 touring and lecturing through England and Scotland. They spoke at large abolition, peace, and temperance gatherings. They also helped organize the pro-Garrisonian Anti-Slavery League for all England. At Bristol in late August Dr. J. B. Estlin, an eye surgeon, took the two Americans to an asylum for the blind; 60 men, women, and children, having recently heard a reading of Douglass's *Narrative*, crowded around them, eager to question and touch the ex-slave.

Satisfied with the results of his tour and Douglass's continued good work, in early November Garrison boarded a steamboat at Liverpool for the return voyage to America. Standing on the dock and waving goodbye as Garrison sailed off, Douglass felt homesick. He had now been away from Anna and his children for nearly 15 months. But could he return without risk of recapture? Abolitionist papers printed reports that his former master had vowed that if Douglass came back he would seize him and "cost what it may . . . place him in the cotton fields of the South." On several occasions British supporters had offered to pay to have his family brought to England and to help establish them there permanently. No doubt the idea of living in a land with neither slavery nor apparent racial prejudice was tempting. Here he had friends and fame. But Douglass realized that his true place was in America. As he told a London audience, though he "had every inducement" to remain in England, "I prefer living a life of activity in the service of my brethren. I choose . . . to return to America." He would share the plight of other black Americans and "struggle in their ranks for that emancipation which shall yet be achieved by the power of truth and principle."

Just a month after Garrison's return, English friends helped make it possible for Douglass to go back by purchasing his freedom. Two Quaker women, Ellen and Anna Richardson of Newcastle, raised the necessary funds and negotiated the sale. Learning that Thomas Auld had transferred ownership of Frederick to his brother, the Richardsons contacted Hugh Auld through American agents. On December 5, 1846, after receiving payment of $711.66 (more than a year's salary for the average American), Hugh Auld signed a deed of manumission stating: "my NEGRO MAN named FREDERICK BAILEY, otherwise called DOUGLASS . . . to be henceforth free, manumitted, and discharged from all manner of servitude." A week later at 10:00 A.M. on December 13, 1846, this paper was duly filed at the Baltimore Chattel Records Office. Frederick Douglass legally became a free man.

His elation over this, however, was somewhat diminished by the wave of controversy that followed. To many abolitionists his purchase was a violation of principles. It implied the legitimacy of selling a human being and that one man could hold another as property. Garrison, who had contributed to Douglass's purchase, defended the deal as an expedient form of "ransom." "We deny," he editorialized, "that purchasing the freedom of a slave is necessarily an implied acknowledgement of the master's right to property in human beings." For nearly three months the argument raged in American abolitionist journals. Some critics even suggested that the purchase had stripped Douglass of his "moral power" to speak "as the representative of the three millions of his countrymen in chains."

In a long letter to Henry Wright, who had recommended that Douglass refuse to accept freedom on these terms, the newly freed slave answered the critics. Published in the *Liberator* of 29 January 1847, Douglass's letter claimed that those opposing his purchase were confusing "the crime of buying men *into slavery*, with the meritorious act of buying men *out of slavery*." Douglass denied that his free status would weaken his will to fight slavery: "I shall be Frederick Douglass still. . . . I shall neither be made to forget nor cease to feel the wrongs of my enslaved fellow-countrymen."

In the long run, of course, it mattered little who got the better of the argument. Douglass at last was legally free and could now return to America. A hectic speaking schedule kept him in England through the winter of 1847. Then on March 30 a public farewell was thrown in his honor. Some 700 "persons of great respectability," including prominent public officials, clergy, journalists, and "very many elegantly dressed ladies," assembled at London Tavern to pay homage to the handsome young American. Some notables such as novelist Charles Dickens, though unable to attend, sent letters of regret. Douglass in turn expressed his regrets at leaving the land where he had been treated "with utmost kindness, with the utmost deference, with the utmost attention."

A few days later Douglass was in Liverpool ready to set sail for Boston. Once again he was to take the *Cambria* and once again he was denied regular accommodations because of his color. Though furious at facing discrimination that he had not encountered in his entire British tour, Douglass was too eager to get home to refuse passage. However, his parting letter to the London *Times* describing the Cunard Line's racist policies caused such a reaction in the press and public that the ship company promised to prohibit such discrimination in the future.

Douglass, in reflecting upon his experiences of the previous 20 months, had much to be proud of: "What a contrast is my *present* with my former condition," he wrote. "Then a slave, now a free man; then degraded, now respected; then ignorant, despised, neglected, unknown, and unfriended, my name unheard of beyond the narrow limits of a republican slave plantation; now, my friends and benefactors, people of *both* hemispheres, to heaven the praise belongs!" His journey had brought him fame, friendship, and freedom. Now, more mature and independent, he was ready and committed to rejoin the fight for freedom in America.

5

THE *NORTH STAR*

O n learning that Douglass was en route to America, William Lloyd Garrison predicted that "he will be warmly welcomed by the Abolitionists, and doubtless, more kindly regarded by people generally, in consequence of the generous and honorable reception given him in Great Britain." This prophecy proved true. Scarcely was Douglass off the boat and rejoining his family when he was swept up in a series of welcome-home festivities. There were gatherings in his hometown of Lynn, in Boston, in New Bedford, and at the meeting of the American Anti-Slavery Society in New York. So many people seemed eager to see and honor the returning freeman that Douglass confessed he could not "attend half the meetings and parties that people are anxious to get up for me."

But what was Douglass's place now to be in the antislavery movement? At the time of his departure for England he was a follower of Garrison and still regarded as something of a "prize exhibit" on the lecture circuit. He had returned his own man, with an international reputation as a magnificent speaker, a brilliant thinker, and a major reformer. Could he simply step back into the old routine?

He himself had new aspirations. To British friends he had confided his desire to launch an antislavery newspaper in

America. So supportive were these associates that they started a subscription fund and raised over $2,000 to assist the project.

Soon after his return the excited Douglass told Garrison and Wendell Phillips his new plan. To his dismay both men advised against it. They gave several practical reasons. The first and foremost was financial. Running a paper was costly and chances of success slim. "The land is full of the wrecks of such experiments," Garrison pointed out. There was also the risk that if Douglass did fail at such a venture this would reflect poorly on his race and limit his future effectiveness. Would it not be better, they argued, for him to continue to lecture? At this he had already proven himself and now with his enhanced reputation his success should be even greater. Finally, Garrison, perhaps not wanting competition with his *Liberator*, two-thirds of whose subscribers were black, claimed there already were enough antislavery papers.

These arguments were not without merit. Certainly the failure rate for reform publications was high, and earlier efforts to establish black-run publications had been short-lived. *Freedom's Journal*, America's first Negro newspaper, began in 1827 and folded early in 1829. Other black publications such as the Reverend Samuel Cornish's *The Colored American*, David Ruggles's *The Mirror of Liberty*, and William Allen's *The National Watchman* lasted somewhat longer, but none survived more than six years.

Black newspaper publishers confronted great problems. There were few black businessmen and professionals to pay for advertisements. Barred by prejudice from high-paying jobs, most free blacks were poor; a newspaper subscription was simply too expensive for many. Previous black editors also had not been able to win the support of white reformers.

Douglass was convinced that there was a real need for a well-edited, black-run publication. Not only would a successful paper reflect creditably on the race, it would also serve an important role in the black community. Though free blacks were appreciative of the work of Garrison and the thousands of other white abolitionists, there were many issues relevant to blacks that white reformers ignored. Blacks possessed a personal and more profound conviction of the need to reform the racist character of American society.

Increasingly segregated from white society and suffering from widespread social, economic, and political discrimination, Northern free blacks were becoming more aware of the need to organize. In the 1830s and 1840s they had begun agitating for change. State and national conventions were held where issues discussed included educational and economic opportunities, political rights, self-improvement, colonization, and other topics of paramount interest to blacks. Douglass had attended a major National Convention of Colored Citizens at Buffalo in 1843. He was well aware of the needs of the free black community. As a Garrisonian abolitionist he primarily dealt with the single issue of slavery and presented himself as a representative of the slaves. As a black newspaper editor, on the other hand, he could address a wider range of topics affecting both slaves and free blacks. He could become the true representative of all American blacks.

Temporarily Douglass gave in to his friends' arguments and abandoned his plan. He agreed to go back to the lecture circuit and in August of 1847 he and Garrison set out to carry "the torch of conscience into dark places of the West." Once again Douglass faced hateful racial prejudice. Many times he was denied service in restaurants; on these occasions he and Garrison both went without food. Taking a train out of Philadelphia, Douglass experienced the humiliation of being dragged from his seat when he refused to sit in a segregated car. At a meeting held in Harrisburg, the capital of Pennsylvania, Douglass's speech was interrupted by a mob throwing firecrackers, stones, hot pepper, and rotten eggs. Only protection provided by a group of blacks in the audience saved Douglass from serious harm.

But the two met with success as well. In great demand, they often lectured several times a day. At a convention of the Western Anti-Slavery Society in New Lynne, Ohio, a gathering of more than 4,000 crowded under a giant tent to hear them. A week later in Salem, Ohio, they were greeted by about 5,000 supporters. "Enthusiasm," exclaimed Garrison, "is unequalled. Opposition to our holy cause seems stunned."

The hectic schedule of traveling in horse-drawn vehicles, speaking in tents, crowded halls, even out of doors in the rain soon took its toll on the two abolitionists. Douglass suffered a severe sore throat and had to cancel several scheduled speeches. Then in Cleveland it was Garrison who collapsed exhausted and with a high fever. Douglass desired to remain with his sick friend, but left reluctantly at Garrison's insistence that he should continue to meet their lecture engagements.

Douglass traveled on to meetings in Buffalo, Rochester, and Syracuse. His addresses were well received, but he was saddened to hear that Garrison remained ill. He reproached himself for having left his friend's side. Through Samuel May, a fellow abolitionist, who was writing to Garrison, Douglass conveyed his concern.

Garrison did slowly recover, but became irritable. In a letter to his wife he complained that Douglass had "not written a single line to me . . . inquiring after my health." Perhaps the real reason for his sudden hostility was something else. Soon after leaving Cleveland, Douglass, without consulting Garrison, revived his plan to start a newspaper. To Garrison this proposal was "impulsive, inconsiderate and highly inconsistent with his decision in Boston." From then on these two great champions of black freedom would never again be friends.

Douglass now quickly set about to implement his cherished scheme. Not wishing to publish anywhere near the already established *Liberator* and its now hostile editor, Douglass chose Rochester. A flourishing city of some 30,000 located along the Erie Canal, Rochester was central to the region of upstate New York known as the "burnt over district" because so many religious revivals had swept through the area. These revivals had helped stimulate interest in reforms such as temperance and abolitionism. When Douglass first appeared in Rochester in 1842 and again in September of 1847, he had been warmly received. The leading abolitionist of the region, Gerrit Smith of nearby Peterboro, was not a Garrisonian. Unlike Garrison, Smith believed slavery could be attacked through the political system rather than relying solely on moral persuasion. Not doctrinaire, the wealthy, philanthropic Smith extended the hand of friendship to Douglass despite the fact that the black abolitionist still considered himself a Garrisonian.

On 1 November 1847 Douglass moved his family into their own nine-room brick house located on the outskirts of Rochester. He had purchased this attractive, two-story home with his earnings as a lecturer. To help start his new career he also had over $2,000 from British supporters and a deed to 40 acres of land outside of Rochester given to him by Gerrit Smith.

That same 1 November there appeared an announcement in the *Ram's Horn*, a black New York City paper, stating that Frederick Douglass proposed to publish a newspaper to be called the *North Star*. The purpose of this paper, the announcement read, "will be to attack slavery in all its forms and aspects; advocate Universal Emancipation . . . promote

The village of Rochester, New York, where Frederick Douglass lived and edited The North Star. From a sketch made in 1827 by a visiting English naval officer, Captain Basil Hall.

the moral and intellectual improvement of the colored people; and to hasten the day of freedom to our three million enslaved fellow-countrymen."

Though perfectly willing to accept the help of whites, Douglass had come to the realization that blacks must take a leading role in advancing their own cause. When the first edition of the *North Star* appeared on 3 December 1847 this position was clearly stated. Douglass expressed "appreciation of the zeal, integrity [and] ability of the noble band of white laborers" on behalf of the enslaved black, but insisted "that the man who has *suffered the wrong* is the man to *demand* redress—*that the man STRUCK is the man to CRY OUT—and that* he who has *endured* the cruel pangs of Slavery *is the man to advocate Liberty.*"

Much of Douglass's life had been a personal declaration of independence: his early dreams of freedom, his learning to read and write, the fight with Covey, his escape from slavery, the British sojourn. Founding the *North Star* was a new declaration of freedom. He would no longer accept a role imposed upon him by others, however well meaning they were. "I shall be under no party of society," he pledged, "but shall advocate the slave's cause in the way which in my judgment, will be best suited to the advancement of the cause."

Douglass's Garrisonian colleagues never fully accepted his need for independence. Though men like Garrison and Phillips were as liberated from the taint of racism as was possible for whites to be in a racist land, even they were not entirely free from prejudice. This was reflected in their paternalistic attitude toward Douglass and other black abolitionists. They presumed to know best what Douglass's role should be. His rejection of their patronizing guardianship struck them as childish insubordination.

Douglass later claimed that he "labored hard to convince them that my way of thinking about the matter was the right one, but without success." This was partly true. Initially at least Douglass tried to remain close to his former associates. However, being only human it was not surprising that he soon reacted to their hostility with resentment. Living in Rochester, he was both physically and emotionally removed from the Boston abolitionists. Soon he not only lost touch with these former friends but began to challenge their political views as well.

In 1840, the year before Douglass officially joined the antislavery movement, American abolitionists had split into two antagonistic factions. The Garrisonians controlled the American Anti-Slavery Society. Their opponents formed the American and Foreign Anti-Slavery Society. To the Garrisonians existing institutions such as the churches and political parties had been hopelessly corrupted by slavery. The Constitution itself, they argued, was a proslavery document that designated a black as only three-fifths of a person. Voting, therefore, should be avoided; it served to encourage the proslavery government. They also preached disunion. So corrupted was the South that only secession could save the North. William Lloyd Garrison thought that it would take a revolution in public opinion and belief to destroy slavery. Like the revivalist preachers of the age, he and his followers hoped to convince people of the moral rightness of immediate emancipation.

The young, unschooled Douglass fresh out of bondage had accepted Garrisonian doctrines as religious truths. Moral suasion, he believed, would carry all before it. "All the American people needed, I thought, was light. Could they know slavery as I knew it, they would hasten to the work of its extinction."

By the 1840s many abolitionists found Garrison's views too extreme and the strategy of moral suasion too limited. Led by such people as Arthur and Lewis Tappan, James Birney, Lysander Spooner, and Gerrit Smith, these abolitionists considered political action essential. The Constitution, they argued, was an antislavery document with the stated purpose of promoting the general welfare and securing the blessings of liberty. They also concluded that disunion was a mistake since it would only place the slaves at the complete mercy of the

South. In 1840 these abolitionists had launched the American and Foreign Anti-Slavery Society as well as the Liberty party to work for political abolition.

While lecturing during the 1840s in both the United States and Great Britain, Douglass had met many political abolitionists. He and Garrison had even debated against some at Oberlin College over the question of whether or not the Constitution was an antislavery document. They had both opposed this interpretation and condemned voting as well. This was still Douglass's position when he began the *North Star* late in 1847. Over the next few years his views changed. His personal feud with the Garrisonians no doubt influenced him. So, too, did living in Rochester, which was a hotbed of political abolitionism. In particular he came under the influence of his new friend and patron, Gerrit Smith. Above all, Douglass's change resulted from his own careful reevaluation of the issues. Writing weekly editorials for his paper forced him to analyze all aspects of the antislavery movement. Such study convinced Douglass of the usefulness of political action.

In May of 1851, at the annual meeting of the American Anti-Slavery Society, Douglass announced his new position. With Garrison in the chair, Douglass told the shocked delegates that he was now convinced the Constitution "might be consistent in its details with the noble purpose avowed in its preamble" where it pledged that the United States was created to "establish Justice, insure domestic Tranquility, provide for the common defence, promote the general Welfare, and secure the Blessings of Liberty to ourselves and our Posterity." He recommended the use of political action along with moral suasion in the fight against slavery.

Furious at this, Garrison muttered from his platform seat just behind Douglass: "There is roguery somewhere." As far as he was concerned Douglass had gone over to the enemy. Garrison's attacks upon Douglass became increasingly personal. Douglass, he wrote, was "destitute of every principle of honor, ungrateful to the last degree, and malevolent in spirit."

For his part, Douglass, though by nature more of a com-promiser than the sectarian Garrison, soon became bitter. "They talk down there," he wrote of the Boston abolitionists, "just as if the Anti-Slavery Cause belonged to them . . . and that no man has a right to 'peep or mutter' on the subject, who does not hold letters patent from them." Northern blacks were forced to take sides. Some, like Douglass's former friend Charles Remond remained loyal Garrisonians and claimed to speak for "all the true colored men in the country." But the majority of free blacks supported Douglass. A Chicago Negro convention, for example, condemned Garrison's "vile crusade" against "the voice of the colored people"; while in Rhode Island a black meeting called Douglass "our acknowledged leader." It was a sad quarrel and reduced the effectiveness of the antislavery movement.

In spite of this, Douglass's journalistic career was soon a success. The pages of his paper contained far more than his disputes with his former supporters. His paper began as the *North Star*, named for the star frequently followed by fugitive slaves fleeing to freedom. In 1851, reflecting Douglass's change of philosophy, the *North Star* merged with the *Liberty Party Paper* that Gerrit Smith had been financing. Henceforth the paper was called *Frederick Douglass's Paper*. In 1858 *Douglass' Monthly* was also launched, largely for British readers. All told Douglass's newspaper venture would run from 1847 until 1863. This was an exciting period, filled with momentous events as the issue of slavery came to a crisis that ultimately culminated in the Civil War. For Douglass, who was near the center of this unfolding drama, these years would turn out to be the most creative and significant of his life.

Douglass had come to see his life as more than a personal matter. As a famous and conspicuous black leader he had to be exemplary for the sake of his race. He brought this attitude to his journalism. Not only was it important that his paper survive, it must also be as good or better than similar white publications. His well-written and well-edited publications would fulfill these high goals.

In format the *North Star* and its successor, *Frederick Douglass' Paper*, were similar to the *Liberator* and other reform papers. The typical weekly edition consisted of four pages with seven columns of text on each page. The front page might report on an antislavery convention, congressional speeches on slavery issues, news of local, national, and international abolitionist societies, and information about other reform movements. The second and sometimes the third page were generally taken up with Douglass's editorials. He also printed clips from other sources, a common editorial practice at that time. These often took up much of the paper's last two pages and could include anything from a temperance speech to a poem by the antislavery poet John Greenleaf Whittier to an excerpt from Charles Dickens's reformist novel *Bleak House*.

Abolitionism and other reforms were not the sole focus of Douglass's paper. Just as important were issues of concern to the free black community apart from antislavery. As a Garrisonian abolitionist Douglass had generally associated with whites. Now as a black editor he became more race conscious, more concerned about the plight of free blacks. Each issue featured reports from black correspondents in various localities. Under the name of "Communipaw," James McCune Smith, a physician and Glasgow University graduate, sent a weekly letter from New York City. William J. Wilson reported from Brooklyn using the pseudonym of "Ethiope." Other important black correspondents whom Douglass encouraged and published included Samuel Ringgold Ward, a fugitive slave writing from Canada; Amos Gerry Beman from New Haven; George T. Downing from Chicago; and William G. Allen, a professor at Central College in McGrawville, New York. These men wrote well. Their articles made important contributions to the development of an aware and informed free black community.

Douglass's editorials were the mainstay of the paper. Week after week, year after year, he turned out thoughtful analyses on a wide range of current national and international issues. As he had already proved with his oratory and his *Narrative*, he possessed a wonderful feeling for language. His writing was clear yet vivid. He could be both forceful and humorous, serious and sonorous. His editorial standards were high whether involving something as weighty as the logic of a generalization or as minor as a typographical error.

Much of Douglass's writing was directed specifically at free blacks, and his most persistent message was the need for his people to improve themselves. Though aware that much of the degradation of the race resulted from discrimination, Douglass firmly believed that blacks could help themselves. If blacks would strive for moral and intellectual improvement they would force whites to realize that their prejudices were baseless. "Come, friends and brethren," ran a typical Douglass editorial, "let us unite firmly to do all that in us lies to improve our condition where we are. Let us sustain our press, and keep our men in the field whose voices are never uplifted in our cause in vain. Let us not run from prejudice and hardships, but meet and overcome them. Let us keep pace with the wheels of American civilization, as the best means within our reach to prevent us from being crushed by it. Let us live savingly, that we may educate our children, and place them in favorable circumstances for maintaining an honorable position in society. Banish forever the withering heresy that our condition here is as good as we can make it, and as good as it ever will be."

As Douglass saw it slaves and free blacks were inextricably bound: freedom for the former was tied to the success of the latter. "To strengthen prejudice against the *free*, he stressed, "is to rivet the fetter more firmly on the slave population." Only through self-improvement could free blacks undermine the prejudice used to justify slavery. Douglass made every effort to publicize black accomplishments. "It is not the least among the good offices of the *North Star* that it searches out and brings to the light of day those of our despised people whose manly characters serve to reflect credit upon themselves and all with whom they are identified." The paper itself, of course, and its famous editor symbolized black achievement.

Douglass's paper could be judged a success by every standard save one: financial. Garrison's and Phillips's warnings had been correct. Keeping a reform publication out of debt was no easy matter. Indeed no pre-Civil War reform paper was ever self-supporting; all had to struggle for survival. Douglass found this out all too quickly. Though he was able to start the paper debt-free thanks mainly to the generosity of his British friends, most of what they gave was spent on a press and other equipment. Within less than a year Douglass had to mortgage his house to help keep the press running. Often the paper contained urgent appeals for money. Douglass also raised funds by making frequent lecture tours where he was able to charge a considerable fee: $25 per speech.

Most helpful in keeping the paper going was the work of an Englishwoman, Julia Griffiths. Douglass first met her during his British tour and they had become close friends. Young, bright, and attractive, Miss Griffiths was dedicated to antislavery and to Douglass. Arriving in Rochester in 1848, she moved into the Douglass home and became the business manager of the paper.

At her suggestion Douglass separated his personal finances from those of the paper. Within a year her tireless work brought the paper out of debt. Largely through her efforts the paper's circulation rose from 2,000 to 4,000 copies. She helped organize antislavery bazaars where goods would be sold to benefit the paper. She launched a national $10 gift campaign. In 1853 she compiled and marketed a collection of antislavery literature, *Autographs for Freedom*. Later in life when paying tribute to those who had aided his newspaper career Douglass wrote that no one was more helpful than "the ever active and zealous friend of the slave, Miss Julia Griffiths."

But Julia Griffiths was more than the paper's imaginative business manager. During these years she was also Douglass's closest friend. She served him in ways that his wife Anna could not. Anna was proud of her husband's success and treated him with great respect. She also was a good mother and a meticulous housekeeper. Yet she remained largely illiterate; she could not share her husband's intellectual life. Julia, on the other hand, was well-educated. She encouraged Douglass's intellectual growth and often read to him at night from the classics. She also helped the self-taught ex-slave with the finer points of grammer and writing style.

Clearly Griffiths and Douglass were fond of one another, though given Douglass's high moral standards it is extremely doubtful that they had anything more than a close friendship and a good working relationship. Nevertheless, there was gossip, and that is not surprising. A black man keeping company in public with a white woman was not acceptable to mid-nineteenth-century white Americans. Simply by associating together, Frederick and Julia defied convention.

Anna, too, became increasingly jealous of the Englishwoman. Under such pressures Julia moved out of the Douglass household in 1852 and three years later returned to Britain. Though she married soon after this and did not return to Rochester, she and Douglass remained close correspondents for more than 40 years.

Next to Griffiths and Douglass himself, the third most important figure in keeping the paper going was Gerrit Smith. Supportive from the first, Smith's generosity increased after Douglass became a political abolitionist. In 1851 when at Smith's suggestion Douglass agreed to merge the *North Star* with the *Liberty Party Paper*, Smith provided a regular subsidy.

This support carried the paper through for a number of years. But by the late fifties depressed conditions spread throughout the North and once again the paper's expenses ran ahead of revenues. Finally in 1860 Douglass was forced to end weekly publication, though he did manage to keep the *Douglass' Monthly* going. That, too, ceased in 1863, the year of the Emancipation Proclamation.

The overall significance of Douglass's 16-year journalistic career was great. His editorial experiences forced him to analyze events and make judgments. He read widely, studied issues, and matured intellectually. Under the weekly pressures of producing a paper not only did his mind expand but so, too, did his sense of power and competence. He became his own man, a truly self-reliant individual, and no longer anyone's protégé. These years were the busiest and most productive of his life. Looking back, Douglass later wrote that "if at any time I have said or written that which is worth remembering or repeating, I must have said such things between the years 1848–1860."

Equally important was the way publishing a newspaper heightened Douglass's sensitivity to the problems of all black Americans, slave and free. His paper was a powerful voice for abolitionism, a major factor in the creation of an informed and racially conscious black community, and the most important publication for black writers and reformers. Publishing made Douglass a true leader of his race. He became concerned with every facet of black life and all aspects of discrimination. Blacks in turn took great pride in Douglass's success. A good indication of this was the following statement in a contemporary black journal *The Rising Sun*: "Frederick Douglass's ability as an editor and publisher has done more for the freedom and elevation of his race than all his platform appearances." This was high praise indeed for one recognized as among the great orators of the age. As he had hoped at the outset, Douglass's journalistic accomplishments had made him a symbol of black achievement and a significant factor in the fight for freedom.

6

"RIGHT IS OF NO SEX"

O n July 14, 1848, Douglass's *North Star* carried the
following announcement:

> A Convention to discuss the Social, Civil and Religious Con-
> dition and Rights of Women, will be held in the Wesleyan
> Chapel at Seneca Falls, New York, on Wednesday and
> Thursday, the 19th and 20th of July instant.

A new reform was about to begin: the struggle for women's
rights. Frederick Douglass would be in the forefront of this
great movement.

Women suffered severe disadvantages in antebellum
America. Like free blacks and minor children, they were
systematically denied even the most elementary rights that
adult white males proclaimed as "natural." Legally they were
denied the right to vote, denied control of their own property
and even of their children. By law a husband could administer
physical punishment to his wife. The wife could not sue in
court, sign a contract, make a will, or, if employed, have
access to her own wages.

Generally, jobs available to women were limited to
domestic service, needlework, textile factory employment,
and elementary schoolteaching. Pay for women in such jobs
was extremely low, frequently averaging less than a dollar per

week, which was far below subsistence level. Women working in the same jobs as men generally earned less than half as
much as male employees. Educational opportunities for
women were also very limited. Beyond learning to read and
write, women might be taught certain domestic skills and
"feminine" graces. Higher education and professional
schools, with but few exceptions, were closed to them.

Most men and women at that time did not see such practices
as discriminatory. They believed women to be very different
from men. It was assumed that either God or biology had
destined women for a "separate sphere." American culture
was permeated with the notion that women's place was in the
home, as wife and mother. "As society is constituted," wrote
the author of an 1846 article on the "Domestic and Social
Claims of Woman," "the true dignity and beauty of the the
female character . . . consists in a right understanding and
faithful and cheerful performance of social and family duties."

Just as proslavery propaganda depicted blacks as childlike
and dependent, so, too, were women portrayed. A typical
view was that God had implanted "the instinct of protection
in man and the instinct of dependence in women." Or as a
later feminist author described the nineteenth-century
woman: "she was the subject creature, and versed in the arts of
the enslaved." Women, it was believed, were by nature more
moral, sentimental, and intuitive than men, but less logical,
original, and vigorous. While in the home women were expected to be the guardians of virtue, the outside world of business and politics was seen as too competitive for the delicate
female character. It was in this sexist environment that the
women's rights movement began.

Since one of the few activities outside the home in which
women were encouraged to take part was religion, it was not
surprising that thousands of women participated in church
activities. But as women were swept up in the great revivals of
the age many also began to take active roles in moral reforms
such as temperance, the peace movement, and especially
abolitionism. In these movements women learned the skills of
organizing, writing, petitioning, and public speaking. They

also became more aware of sexual prejudice, particularly when they spoke in public.

Sarah and Angelina Grimké were important abolitionists during the 1830s. Sisters who had grown up in a South Carolina slaveholding family, they moved North and began denouncing slavery from the lecture platform. Like Douglass, the Grimkés helped give authenticity to abolitionist charges. Many people were outraged by their lectures, not just because they opposed slavery, but simply because they were women who dared to speak in public. The Massachusetts Council of Congregationalist Ministers went so far as to publish an official Pastoral Letter warning of "the dangers which at present seem to threaten the female character with widespread and permanent injury" when a woman took on a role unbecoming "the modesty of her sex."

The harsh opposition that the Grimkés encountered was for them a radicalizing experience. They came to see a direct link between the position of slaves and that of women. In 1838 Sarah Grimké authored *The Equality of the Sexes and the Condition of Women*, the first feminist treatise published by an American woman. "God," she asserted, "has made no distinction between men and women as moral beings."

As women like the Grimkés became active in the abolitionist movement, the question of the status of women came to the fore. Not only were women activists meeting with hostility from those opposed to abolitionism, but even many males within the antislavery movement felt that women's presence damaged the cause. In May of 1840 at the annual meeting of the American Anti-Slavery Society, the election of female abolitionist Abby Kelley to the executive committee triggered the split within the movement. Though the question of political participation was paramount, it was the insistence of the Garrisonians that women be treated equally within the movement that proved the pivotal point in the break. To most of those who separated from Garrison to form the American and Foreign Anti-Slavery Society the issue of women's rights was "excess baggage" that threatened to distract people from the fight against slavery.

Later that year at the World Anti-Slavery Convention in London the "women question" again came to a head. After bitter debate the convention voted not to seat the female delegates. Among the American women forced to sit passively in a curtained-off gallery during the 10-day convention were veteran Quaker abolitionist Lucretia Mott and the young bride of an antislavery leader and cousin of Gerrit Smith, Elizabeth Cady Stanton. This meeting in banishment cemented a friendship and created a cause. Henceforth, Mott and Stanton would place the rights of women first.

Back in Boston where Stanton was living in the early 1840s she worked hard to win over antislavery people to feminism. One of her first and most notable converts was Frederick Douglass. As he recalled she was "at pains of setting before me in a very strong light the wrong and injustice" of women's exclusion from politics. "I could not meet her arguments except with the shallow plea of 'custom,' 'natural division of duties,' 'indelicacy of woman's taking part in politics,' the common talk of 'woman's sphere,' and the like, all of which that able woman . . . brushed away by those arguments . . . which no man has yet successfully refuted."

Douglass was predisposed to favor women's rights not only because of Stanton's persuasiveness, but also because of the great work "of the honorable women, who have not only assisted me, but who according to their opportunity and ability, have generously contributed to the abolition of slavery, and the recognition of the equal manhood of the colored race." During the 1840s Douglass often appeared on the lecture platform with such women as Abby Kelley and the former slave Sojourner Truth. He knew of the Grimkés and of the editor of the *Anti-Slavery Standard*, Lydia Maria Child. Throughout Douglass's whole life women had played vital roles—Betsey, his beloved grandmother, the kindly Lucretia and Sophia Auld, his wife Anna, Ellen and Anna Richardson, who arranged to buy his freedom, and his loyal friend Julia Griffiths. By 1847 when Douglass established himself in Rochester he fully identified with the budding women's movement. From the first issue the *North Star* carried the bold masthead:

RIGHT IS OF NO SEX—TRUTH IS OF NO COLOR.

By then the movement was gaining momentum. In addition to the work of people such as Mott and Stanton, other women had circulated petitions to try to get state legislatures to change laws regarding the property rights of married women. There were also feminist books such as Margaret Fuller's important *Women in the Nineteenth Century* (1845). But the movement still lacked a coherent, agreed-upon program. This was provided at the first women's rights convention held on July 19 and 20, 1848, in the small upstate New York town of Seneca Falls.

Stanton and her family had moved to Seneca Falls about the same time that Douglass and his family settled in Rochester. She and Lucretia Mott had discussed holding a meeting on the position of women ever since they first met. Now in the early summer of 1848 they put that plan into effect. In order to have

Anna Douglass in middle life. She bore Douglass five children and raised his family. Her service did much to make possible his career.

a program to present they spent several days prior to the meeting drawing up a Declaration of Sentiments. Stanton suggested a paraphrase of the Declaration of Independence, thus connecting the women's cause with the struggle for liberty in the Revolution:

> We hold these truths to be self-evident: that all men and women are created equal. . . .
> The history of mankind is the history of repeated injuries and usurpations on the part of man toward woman, having in direct object the establishment of an absolute tyranny over her.

There followed a list of 18 grievances against Man. These attacked the whole structure of discrimination: legal, educational, economic, social, and political. Some of these read as follows:

> He has compelled her to submit to laws, in the formation of which she had no voice.
> He has taken from her all right in property, even to the wages she earns.
> He has monopolized nearly all the profitable employments, and from those she is permitted to follow, she receives but a scanty remuneration. . . .
> He has denied her the facilities for obtaining a thorough education, all colleges being closed against her.
> He has created a false public sentiment by giving to the world a different code of morals for men and women. . . .
> He has endeavored, in every way that he could, to destroy her confidence in her own powers, to lessen her self-respect, and to make her willing to lead a dependent and abject life.

To remedy these grievances the document listed a series of resolutions to create greater equality between men and women. The most controversial of these was the demand for woman's suffrage as an "inalienable right." Though Elizabeth Cady Stanton was strongly in favor of this, many feminists, including Lucretia Mott, feared such a radical proposal would make the entire movement look ridiculous. Seeking an ally to help her on this issue, Stanton sought the support of

Douglass. As she later put it: "I knew Frederick, from personal experience, was just the man for the work." He readily consented.

When the Seneca Falls meeting opened on July 19, a surprising 300 people were in attendance, including 40 men, among them Douglass. As expected, the suffrage resolution generated heated debate and appeared doomed. But then Douglass, who had seconded Stanton's resolution, took the floor and gave a magnificent speech in favor of the motion. "The power to choose rulers and make laws," he argued, "is the right by which all others could be secured." Douglass's eloquence swayed enough of the wavering to carry the suffrage plank by a bare majority; all other resolutions passed unanimously.

From this first women's convention in 1848 until his death in 1895, Douglass devoted considerable attention to women's rights. But throughout his long career as a "women's rights man" he remained most proud of his pivotal role in supporting suffrage at Seneca Falls. In 1888 at a Woman Suffrage Association meeting Douglass spoke of his having been "sufficiently enlightened" to champion Stanton's resolution: "I have done very little in this world in which to glory except this one act—and I certainly glory in that. When I ran away from slavery, it was for myself; when I advocated emancipation, it was for my people; but when I stood up for the rights of woman, self was out of the question, and I found a little nobility in the act.

The week following the Seneca Falls Convention, Douglass announced in the *North Star* his unequivocal support of "the grand movement for attaining the civil, social, political, and religious rights of women." To him the struggles for the rights of women and blacks were identical. Women, according to some males, were legally and politically represented through their fathers or husbands. But as Douglass saw it, men could no more legitimately exercise the rights of women than whites could exercise the rights of blacks. Rights and respect went together; to be deprived of the former was to be denied the latter. Only full freedom to participate equally in all aspects of politics and society could give women and blacks not only the rights but the respect that was their due.

Two weeks after the Seneca Falls gathering, Douglass attended a second women's rights meeting in his hometown of Rochester. Again he spoke in favor of women's suffrage claiming "that the only true basis of right was the capacity of the individuals." A little over a year later he was present at the first national Woman's Rights Convention held in Worcester, Massachusetts. There he urged "woman to take her rights as far as she can get them." Reflecting the close ties between abolitionism and women's rights, this convention adopted the motto: "Equality before the law without distinction of sex or color."

Douglass, Garrison, and other abolitionists wholeheartedly supported the women's movement; public reaction, however, was generally hostile. The *New York Herald*, in a typically vitriolic article on the Worcester convention, headlined its account: "Awful Combination of Socialism, Abolitionism, and Infidelity." Scoffing at the notion that a woman could hold political office, the *New York Mirror* charged that "woman's offices are those of wife, mother, daughter, sister, friend—Good God, can they not be content with these?"

Such abuse did not dissuade the dedicated people who flocked to the women's cause. With the abolitionist movement as a model, feminists used the tactics of public propaganda, political lobbying, and petition. Except for 1857, national women's rights conventions were held yearly from 1850 to 1860. There were also numerous state and local gatherings. At many of these meetings Frederick Douglass was a featured speaker. He also used his paper to further this cause. In a typical 1853 editorial he asserted that "a woman should have every honorable motive to exertion which is enjoyed by man, to the full extent of her capacities and endowments. The case is too plain for argument. Nature has given woman the same powers, and subjected her to the same earth, breathes the same air, subsists on the same food, physical, moral, mental and spiritual. She has, therefore, an equal right with man, in all efforts to obtain and maintain a perfect existence." In addition to his frequent feminist editorials, Douglass also opened his paper to women writers and printed announcements and reports on women's rights meetings.

While Douglass fully supported the women's movement, as with his other reform activities he brought a black perspective to the cause. Mid-nineteenth-century feminism was primarily a white, middle-class movement; he worried that on occasion white feminists were advancing their interests without due regard to slave women. "Other women suffer certain wrongs," he chided the women's rights leaders, "but the wrongs peculiar to woman out of slavery, great and terrible as they are, are endured as well by the slave woman who has also to bear the ten thousand wrongs of slavery in addition to the common wrongs of woman."

Douglass was consistent. When famed Negro soprano Elizabeth Greenfield performed at New York's Metropolitan Hall before an audience from which blacks had been excluded, he publicly criticized the great contralto. Known as the "Black Swan," Douglass dubbed Greenfield the "Black Raven." Stung by this criticism, the singer agreed to perform a benefit concert to aid black charities. In various ways, therefore, Douglass helped keep the women's movement sensitive to issues of racial prejudice.

From Seneca Falls to the Civil War the movement grew. Women faced ridicule as they battled for equal rights. The struggle was not an easy one, but the movement did begin to win some tangible victories. In 1848, after extensive petition drives, the New York Legislature passed the Married Women's Property Law, giving women some control over their wages, income, and property. In the years before the Civil War a number of other Northern states followed the New York example. Feminists also succeeded in pressuring several states to modify divorce laws to the benefit of women.

In another area the women's movement fought the notion that the female constitution was too frail to withstand the rigors of Greek, mathematics, and other branches of higher learning. As early as 1837, Oberlin College in Ohio, founded by abolitionists, began to admit both women and blacks. By the time of the Civil War a few other institutions had followed Oberlin's example, though educational opportunities for women and blacks remained limited.

An additional gain that the movement helped to win was the acceptance of women as public speakers. Though sometimes silenced and often heckled, by the 1850s women active in the reform movements had generally won the right to speak.

A few determined women also forced their way into previously all-male professions. In 1849 feminist Elizabeth Blackwell became the first American woman to graduate from a medical school. Three years later Oberlin graduate Antoinette Brown was the first woman ordained as a minister. Other women such as Amelia Bloomer, Paulina Wright Davis, and Jane Swisshelm edited feminist periodicals.

Such achievements, unfortunately, were uncommon. Prejudice and bigotry continued to keep most women in a subordinate and dependent state. By the time of the Civil War most feminists had come to agree with Stanton and Douglass that only the ballot could open the door to true equality for women. To Douglass women's dignity and power were directly related to their right to vote: "power," he claimed, "is the highest object of human respect. . . . To deny woman her vote is to abridge her natural and social power, and deprive her of a certain measure of respect. Everybody knows that a woman's opinion of any lawmaker would command a larger measure of attention had she the means of making opposition effective at the ballot box."

Douglass believed that all just governments must rest on the consent of the people governed. Since the American government deprived women of the vote it lacked their consent and consequently was not a legitimate government. "Our government," he observed "is in its essence, a simple usurpation, a Government of force, and not of reason. We legislate for woman, and protect her, precisely as we legislate for and protect animals, asking the consent of neither." Like most nineteenth-century Americans, Douglass believed that women possessed superior moral and intuitive perceptions.

These feminine virtues, he argued, should be put to good use in governing the nation: "a government by man alone is at best a half supplied government. it is like a bird with only one wing—floundering to earth unable to soar . . . to the highest and best."

Douglass was aware that the struggle for women's rights was a social reform with far-reaching implications. The achievement of sexual equality, he wrote, would be "a revolution, the most strange, radical, and stupendous that the world has ever witnessed." But he remained more a *political* than a *social* feminist. To him the liberation of women did not mean abandonment of their traditional roles as wives and mothers. His marriage to Anna followed the customary pattern of the age. He was the protector and breadwinner; her duties were to keep the home and raise the family.

Douglass revealed very little about his private life in his autobiographies and scarcely mentioned Anna and his children. It appears to have been a less than ideal marriage. The Douglasses had five children: Rosetta, Lewis, Frederick Jr., and Charles born between 1839 and 1844 in Massachusetts, and a second daughter, Annie, born in Rochester in 1849. The early years were a period of financial hardship as the young couple struggled to support themselves and their growing family. During this period Anna often supplemented the family income by working as a household servant and taking in washing. She was a good cook and an able housekeeper.

Beginning in 1841, when Douglass was hired by the Massachusetts Anti-Slavery Society, their lives changed. Douglass became a public figure and often spent months at a time away from home. His first trip to England in the mid-1840s separated him from his family for nearly two years. During these years Douglass was growing both intellectually and in public stature. Increasingly he and Anna lived in separate worlds.

Anna was proud of her husband's achievements and he certainly appreciated her abilities as a homemaker and mother. Otherwise they had little in common. While

Douglass delighted to be in the presence of prominent people of both races, his wife was ill at ease in such company. In the words of Rosetta, her mother was "not well versed in the polite etiquette of the drawing-room." Douglass often invited dignitaries to their Rochester home. On such occasions Anna cooked, served the meals, and then withdrew, leaving her husband to entertain the guests. Douglass was away so frequently that his homecomings were important events: "Father was an honored guest of mother," Rosetta recalled.

In 1849, at Douglass's insistance, a tutor was hired for Anna. The experiment failed. Anna remained unable to read or write effectively and thus was cut off from the larger world of her husband. The couple shared in the raising of their children, but here, too, Douglass was away so much that this task fell mostly to Anna. Certainly Douglass loved his children, but like many public figures he chose to sacrifice the family for what he considered his larger mission in life.

Like all respectable nineteenth-century Americans, Douglass saw the family as the keystone of civilization. In his newspaper editorials and speeches directed at black audiences he often stressed the need for stable families as essential to furthering the progress of the race. His own marriage was not, in any modern sense, a marriage of equals.

Despite the limitations of Douglass's feminism when it came to his personal life, his efforts to challenge male supremacy were advanced for the age. From the Seneca Falls meeting in 1848 until his death in 1895 he played an important role in the women's movement. He attended numerous conventions, made many speeches, and wrote various articles in support of sexual equality. It would take another generation of struggle after Douglass's death for women to gain the vote; even today women have yet to achieve full equality. But the great advances that women have made in the twentieth century are due in no small measure to the efforts of pioneering, nineteenth-century feminists such as Frederick Douglass.

7

"THE BEES WILL BEGIN TO SWARM"
Douglass and John Brown

Nearly a year before the Seneca Falls Convention Frederick Douglass met John Brown. This took place in the fall of 1847, and was of great consequence for both men. Douglass was busy that fall moving his family to Rochester and making preparations to launch the *North Star*. But amidst this hectic schedule, while lecturing in New England he accepted an invitation to spend an evening with John Brown. Though he did not know Brown personally, several times since his return from England he had heard prominent blacks mention his name, and when they spoke of him, Douglass noted, "their voices would drop to a whisper, and what they said of him made me very eager to see and to know him."

Brown for his part was just as anxious to meet Douglass. He had been following the former slave's remarkable career with special interest. Brown was a white man and, like Douglass, fully committed to the crusade against slavery. Indeed Douglass later described him as being "as deeply interested in our cause as though his own soul had been pierced with the iron of slavery." Brown had a secret plan to end slavery and was eager to enlist Douglass's support. He foresaw a special role for the black leader.

The two men first met at Brown's place of business sometime in November of 1847. At the time Brown was a wool merchant in Springfield, Massachusetts. From his warehouse they made their way to Brown's home, an unpretentious dwelling in a working-class neighborhood. There Douglass was warmly received by Brown's wife and children and given an ample, if simple, meal before the two men adjourned to another room to discuss slavery.

To Douglass, Brown appeared "lean, strong, and sinewy, of the best New England mold, built for times of trouble and fitted to grapple with the flintiest of hardships." Douglass was 29 and already recognized as America's most prominent black; Brown was 47 and, except in the wool trade, largely obscure. Nevertheless, it was a meeting of giants with major historical repercussions.

Brown began the discussion hesitantly, perhaps wary of Douglass's reactions. But as he proceeded he became more animated, his bluish-gray eyes filling with "light and fire." Suddenly he exclaimed that "slaveholders had forfeited their right to live."

This bold statement aroused Douglass's interest. He knew at once that he was in the presence of an extraordinary individual. Emboldened by the brightening look in the exslave's eyes, the older man continued. Slavery was a state of war. Slaves had a perfect right to free themselves by any means. Present abolitonist tactics, Brown told Douglass, were inadequate. Neither the Garrisonian doctrine of moral suasion nor political action would abolish the evil system.

What tactic then would succeed? At this point Brown began revealing his plan to Douglass. I "am not averse to shedding blood," he said, for "no people could have self-respect, or be respected who would not fight for their freedom." He quickly assured Douglass, however, that he did not "contemplate a general rising among the slaves, and a general slaughter of the slave-masters." Such a bloodletting would defeat the purpose, and besides there was no way that John Brown or anyone else could organize rapidly a general uprising of the hugely dispersed, unorganized slaves. What he did envision was the creation of a small, armed, guerrilla force to operate in the very heart of the slaveholding South.

Here Brown unfolded a map of the United States and pointed to the Appalachian range running some 1,200 miles from Maine to Georgia. "These mountains," he said, "are the basis of my plan. God has given the strength of the hills to freedom; they were placed here for the emancipation of the Negro race; they are full of natural forts, where one man for defense will be equal to a hundred for attack; they are full also of good hiding-places, where large numbers of brave men could be concealed, and baffle and elude pursuit for a long time. I know these mountains well, and could take a body of men into them and keep them there despite all the efforts of Virginia to dislodge them."

The purpose of the guerrilla force, he told Douglass, would be "to destroy the money value of slave property, and that can be done by rendering such property insecure." He would start small with about 25 carefully chosen, trained, and armed men. In groups of five on a line of 25 miles these brave men would venture forth from the mountains and seek recruits from amongst the boldest able-bodied slaves. Once the original force had grown to 100 or more the operation would be expanded. By a series of raids on nearby plantations large numbers of slaves could be led to the mountain hideaways. The heartiest volunteers would swell the ranks of the insurgent force and allow the operation to be further extended. Others in increasingly larger numbers would be guided to freedom in the North and Canada.

Douglass had listened to Brown's plan with rapt attention. His practical nature led him to raise some questions: How would the guerrillas subsist? Would the slaveholders not follow the raiders with bloodhounds, surround them with troops, and thus destroy them? Would it not be better to try to persuade the slaveholders by non-violent means to give up their bondsmen?

This last question led Brown to exclaim that the proud slaveholders "would never be induced to give up their slaves, until they felt a big stick about their heads." Brown also dismissed Douglass's other doubts. The mountains would provide protection and once the guerrillas had defeated one force, others "would be careful how they pursued." But even if the entire scheme should fail, "what of it?" concluded Brown: "I can think of no better use for my life than to lay it down in the cause of the slave."

Sensing the older man's absolute sincerity, Douglass was deeply moved. Despite his continuing doubts, he knew the plan had much to recommend it. From that day forward, he later wrote, "my utterances became more tinged by the color of this man's strong impressions." He parted from Brown's house the next day certain that he had never been "in the presence of a stronger religious influence."

John Brown was also greatly affected by the visit. He had long been looking for black men who "possessed the energy of head and heart to demand freedom for their whole people." In Douglass he saw such a figure, an individual whose abilities equaled or surpassed those of any white person and whose leadership, if enlisted in Brown's planned insurrection, might help to assure its success. The result, he now had reason to hope, "must be the downfall of slavery."

At the time of this meeting with Brown, Douglass still believed in Garrison's ideas. In addition to reliance on the power of persuasion, Garrisonian abolitionists were also pacifists. They rejected all use of physical force, no matter how righteous the cause. Douglass could not support this philosophy of "non-resistance" and accept Brown's idea that violence was a necessary part of the abolition movement.

In looking back, however, it is clear that even as a follower of Garrison in the early 1840s, Douglass's professed pacifism was accepted as a tactic, not as an end in itself. In 1843, for instance, when in Pendleton, Indiana, a violent mob felled his friend William White, Douglass had not hesitated to grab a club and rush into the fray. Two years later in writing his autobiography, Douglass described his fight with the slave-breaker Covey in positive and even religious terms. It was "the turning-point in my career as a slave" because it "revived within me a sense of my own manhood. . . . It was a glorious resurrection from the tomb of slavery to the heaven of freedom." Obviously Douglass was not opposed to the use of force in self-defense. From this position it was not a large jump to the acceptance of Brown's doctrine that slavery was a state of war to be opposed by force.

When Douglass began his career as an abolitionist in 1841 he was fired with idealism. On first hearing Garrison speak he was sure that the abolition of slavery was imminent: "So clear were his utterances, so simple and truthful, and so adapted, I conceived, to the human heart were the principles propounded by him, that I thought five years . . . would be all that would be required for the abolition of slavery. I thought it was only necessary for the slaves, or their friends, to lift up the hatchway of slavery's infernal hold, to uncover the bloody scenes of American thraldom, and give the nation a peep into its horrors, its deeds of deep damnation, to arouse them to almost frenzied opposition to this foul curse."

By the time he met Brown in 1847, Douglass had become somewhat pessimistic. Years of being "pelted by the mob, insulted by the crowds, shunned by the Church, denounced by the ministry, ridiculed by the press, spit upon by the loafers" convinced him "that I might perhaps live, struggle, and die, and go down to my grave, and the slaves of the South yet remain in their chains." Peaceful persuasion had not worked the hoped-for miracle. Douglass was ready to explore new tactics. This made him more receptive to Brown's analysis. He continued his peaceful antislavery work after his meeting with Brown, but his faith in Garrisonian principles was weakening. No longer would he place exclusive hope on arguments, prayers and appeals as the way to break the slave's chains.

It was at this time that he launched the *North Star* and began to look toward political action as a means to end slavery. But he also came to have doubts that slavery could ever be abolished by any peaceful process. He first expressed this position shortly after his meeting with Brown, when he shocked a gathering of Garrisonian abolitionists at Salem, Ohio, by declaring that "slavery could only be destroyed by bloodshed." A few months later he editorialized that slaveholders had "no rights more than any other thief or pirate. They have forfeited the right to live, and if the slave should put every one of them to the sword to-morrow, who dare pronounce the penalty disproportionate to the crime, or say that the criminals deserved less than death at the hands of their long-abused chattels?" In May of 1849 he told an astounded crowd at Boston's historic Faneuil Hall that he would welcome the news "that the slaves had risen in the South."

It was not just the persuasiveness of John Brown and disillusionment with Garrison that had convinced Douglass to take a more militant stand. Major historical events from the mid-1840s through the 1850s also pushed him in that direction. Late in 1845 the United States annexed the slaveholding Republic of Texas. Partly as a result of this, in 1846 the U.S. declared war on Mexico. To abolitionists this war, which lasted until 1848, had, in Douglass' words, "no higher or holier motive than that of upholding and propagating slavery." It was a "a war against freedom, against the Negro, and against the interests of the workingmen of this country."

Northerners in general took alarm at the prospect of several new slave states being created from former Mexican territory. Even before the war with Mexico was over, Congressman David Wilmot of Pennsylvania introduced an amendment to a military appropriation bill calling for a prohibition of slavery in any area acquired from Mexico. This Wilmot Proviso passed in the House of Representatives, where the more populous Northern states had a majority. But it was defeated in the more heavily Southern, more proslavery Senate. Many Northerners now came to feel as Douglass and the abolitionists had long felt: the South had too strong a voice in national government.

By mid-century sectional disputes threatened the very existence of the Union. Alarmed at this, moderates in Congress, led by Senator Henry Clay, made a series of proposals intended to satisfy both North and South. Known collectively as the Compromise of 1850, after lengthy and often heated debate it passed in September 1850. To appease the North, California was admitted as a free state and the slave trade, not slavery itself, was ended in Washington, D.C.

The most important concession to the South was a Fugitive Slave Law that gave to the federal government authority to seize fugitive slaves and to send them South, if necessary under federal guard. Mere onlookers were required to help the federal authorities arrest fugitives if asked to; refusal to do so could be punished by imprisonment.

Though the Compromise of 1850 for a time averted an outright split between North and South, neither section was satisfied by this measure. In the North it roused a new mood of popular resistance, a growing conviction that slaveholders dominated the national government and, indeed, threatened its very survival. Douglass was speaking for many people when he said that slavery "in the pride of its power . . . threatens to bring down . . . the American Union."

Events during the 1850s confirmed this conclusion. In 1854 Congress passed the Kansas-Nebraska Act. This highly controversial measure created a new Kansas Territory west of Missouri, overturned the congressional ban on slavery in that area, and opened it up to settlers bringing slaves. Douglass and millions of other free Americans had yet another proof that the government was controlled by the Slave Power. This act, Douglass wrote, "was designed to extend and perpetuate slavery. . . . Slavery aims at absolute sway, and to banish liberty from the country." Divisions between North and South intensified, and Kansas was soon rent by conflict.

Then in 1857 the Supreme Court handed down a decision in the *Dred Scott* case declaring that blacks had been held "so far inferior that they had no rights which the white man was bound to respect." Blacks in other words, whether free or slave, could never be citizens of the United States unless the white community adopted a constitutional amendment conferring citizenship rights. *Dred Scott* further stipulated that Congress had no constitutional right to prohibit slavery in any territory.

Douglass along with Northern abolitionists everywhere denounced this "demoniacal" decision that pledged the government "to support, defend, and propagate the crying curse of human bondage." Southern ascendancy in the national government seemed complete, making the future appear bleak for blacks. The Northern black community experienced a profound sense of despair over ever achieving real freedom and equality in the United States. Some black leaders even began to advocate emigration. The only solution to the problems confronting American Negroes, they argued, was to leave America and create their own state, either in Africa or in the Caribbean.

Douglass was equally upset, but he was no quitter and had no intention of abandoning the slave's cause. "This very attempt to blot out forever the hopes of an enslaved people," he argued, "may be one necessary link in the chain of events preparatory to the downfall and complete overthrow of the whole slave system." He would continue the work of propaganda and political agitation, but if the slaves should resort to violence he would give them his support: the slave, he said, "may learn to fight the devil with fire, and for one, I am in no frame of mind to pray that this may be long deferred."

Throughout these years of intensifying sectional and racial hatred Douglass and John Brown remained friends and allies for freedom. Following their first meeting in 1847 they visited each other on a number of occasions. They also corresponded. On January 9, 1854, for instance, while the Kansas-Nebraska bill was being debated in Congress, Brown wrote to Douglass condemning the "malignant" politicians who supported this "most abominably wicked and injust" law. It was time, he concluded, to stop the corruption of "our truly republican and democratic institutions" by the evil supporters of slavery. Douglass printed this letter in *Frederick Douglass' Paper*.

Almost at once following the passage of the Kansas-Nebraska Act in late May of 1854, Kansas Territory became a battleground between pro- and antislavery forces. Moving in from bordering Missouri and other parts of the South, slaveholders established the Lecompton Constitution in 1855. By the terms of this document one could receive the death penalty for helping slaves to escape or even for saying or writing anything against slavery. A reign of terror was launched as free settlers were waylaid, stripped of their possessions, lashed, and left for dead along the trials. This campaign of violence climaxed in May 1856 when a proslavery mob of nearly a thousand men invaded, sacked, and burned the free-state settlement of Lawrence.

Free-state settlers fought back. Among them were the five sons of John Brown, who arrived in the territory in the spring of 1855; and John Brown himself, who joined them at the end of the year. A few days after the sacking of Lawrence, Brown and a small group, including four of his sons, took revenge by murdering five unarmed men at the tiny proslavery settlement of Pottawatomie. Civil war then broke out in Kansas and raged throughout the summer and fall of 1856.

Brown's willingness to use violence in the cause of freedom was proven in Kansas. But he never lost sight of his original plan to strike a blow against slavery in the very heart of the slaveholding South. By late 1857 when it became clear that the free settlers had won the battle for Kansas, Brown decided it was time to return East.

In January 1858 he appeared on Douglass's doorstep in Rochester. Though Brown assured his host he would not remain long, he stayed for nearly a month. While there Brown busied himself writing letters to supporters, asking for money. He also drew up a Provisional Constitution for a new free state he now proposed to create in the Southern mountains after he had invaded them. He talked incessantly with Douglass about his plan. But although he was cearly obsessed with his scheme and could talk of nothing else from the first thing in the morning until late at night, nevertheless, he left Douglass in the dark about the precise point of attack. Despite this, Douglass did promise to assist his old friend in raising funds and recruits in the free black communities of the North.

The two men also planned a future meeting. This was held in Philadelphia on March 11, 1858, where Brown and his son John Jr. conferred with Douglass and two other black leaders, Henry Highland Garnet and William Still. Brown was still vague about his scheme. But he intended to strike later that spring. In a letter to Douglass that April Brown wrote: "I expect to need all the help I can get by the first of May."

Treachery, however, delayed Brown's plans for more than a year. Hugh Forbes, an English soldier-of-fortune whom Brown had hired to train his recruits, threatened to expose Brown's plan. This caused Brown's major, secret, financial backers, including Gerrit Smith, to advise postponement. Reluctantly Brown agreed and soon returned to Kansas.

Nearly a year later he was back in the East, now with a price on his head for having helped lead some Missouri slaves to freedom. In April 1859 he again stopped in Rochester to talk with Douglass. Brown was now determined to launch an invasion of the South in a more dramatic fashion than merely posting forces in the mountains. He envisioned a daring raid on the government arsenal at Harper's Ferry, Virginia. This act, he assumed, would boldly announce to slaves and slaveholders alike that the war for liberation had begun. A deeply religious man, Brown believed that God had chosen him as His instrument to strike freedom's first blow.

The old man, now grizzled, bearded, and weather-beaten from his years of Kansas fighting, still had Douglass definitely in mind as a key figure in his plan. In their April meeting he was secretive and failed to reveal the full scope of his new scheme. But in early August of 1859 he sent Douglass an urgent message to meet him south of Chambersburg, Pennsylvania, where Brown was staying in a farmhouse about four miles from Harper's Ferry. Douglass traveled there with Shields Green, a runaway slave whom the black leader had been sheltering. Brown, accompanied by John Kagi, a young white who had served with him in Kansas, arranged a secret rendezvous at an old stone quarry. There amidst the boulders the two blacks and Kagi listened as the resolute captain told of his plan to seize the government arsenal at Harper's Ferry.

Douglass was taken by surprise. He had assumed that Brown's plan was to use mountain-based forces to run off slaves just as he had proposed 12 years earlier at Springfield.

This new proposal struck him as "fatal"; he vehemently opposed it. To attack a federal arsenal, he argued, "would array the whole country against us." Brown's description of Harper's Ferry, a spit of land where the Shenandoah River flowed into the Potomac, convinced Douglass that Brown would be "going into a perfect steel trap, and that once in he would never get out alive." Brown countered this by saying he would take hostages and thus would be able "to dictate terms of egress from the town." To this the astonished Douglass replied "that Virginia would blow him and his hostages sky-high, rather than that he should hold Harper's Ferry an hour."

And so the debate raged through all of Saturday and part of Sunday. In Douglass's words it was "Brown for Harper's Ferry, and I against it—he for striking a blow which should instantly rouse the country, and I for the policy of gradually . . . drawing off the slaves to the mountains."

In a final effort to win over his friend, Brown put his arms about the black leader and said: "Come with me, Douglass; I will defend you with my life. I want you for a special purpose. When I strike, the bees will begin to swarm, and I shall want you to help hive them."

Though deeply moved by "the dear old man's eloquence," Douglass made it clear he could not join such a venture. This was not an easy decision for Douglass to make. He was no coward, but he was reluctant to become part of an attack he was sure would fail. No doubt, too, Douglass believed he could serve the cause better in other ways. Turning to Shields Green, he said he was leaving and asked his friend what he had decided to do. Green, who had scarcely spoken during the two-day meeting, clearly stated: "I b'leve I'll go wid de ole man." They quickly parted: Douglass for Rochester and a continued career of leadership; Brown, Kagi, and Shields on the fateful course that took them to Harper's Ferry. Douglass and Brown, these two great foes of slavery, never saw each other again.

Both men's prophecies proved true. When Brown and his band of 18 men, five of them blacks, marched to Harper's

Ferry on the night of October 16, 1859, they were able to seize the arsenal. But, as Douglass had warned, it was a death trap. Militiamen and townspeople soon had them surrounded. Though four of Brown's men managed to escape, Kagi, two of Brown's sons, and seven others were killed outright; on the morning of October 18th Brown surrendered to the commander of the federal forces, Colonel Robert E. Lee. A trial was hastily held, and on 2 December John Brown was hanged. In the following weeks Shields Green and the others met that same fate.

Yet though Brown's plan failed to free the slaves, on another level his daring raid succeeded magnificently. He had told Douglass he wished to do "something startling" in an effort "to rouse the nation." Harper's Ferry, he had predicted, would be as a trumpet blast to rally the friends of freedom. It did just that. Brown's attack, as Douglass later noted, "began the war that ended American slavery and made this a free Republic."

In death Brown quickly became a martyr; when the Civil War commenced Northern soldiers marched to battle singing

> John Brown's body lies a moldering in the grave.
> John Brown's body lies a moldering in the grave.
> John Brown's body lies a moldering in the grave.
> His truth goes marching on!

Not surprisingly the view of John Brown as a great martyr for freedom was, and still is held, most fervently by black Americans. Frederick Douglass was no exception. In 1881 Douglass gave an oration on Brown at Storer College, a black school set up after the Civil War on a hill overlooking the site where the old armory at Harper's Ferry had stood until destroyed during the war. Present on the platform with Douglass was Andrew Hunter, the attorney who in 1859 had prosecuted the case against Brown for the state of Virginia.

It was a spring morning, late in May. "I have come here to talk to you," Douglass told the students, "to pay a just debt long due, to vindicate in some degree a great historical character of our own time and country, . . . whose friendship and confidence it was my good fortune to share, . . . a grand, brave and good old man. I come above all," he added, "so that you may better understand the meaning of the Harper's Ferry raid."

Douglass then reminded his listeners of the facts of that "strange and bloody drama." The small band of men, black and white, who invaded the armory, "collected about fifty slaves, put bayonets into the hands of such as were able and willing to fight for their liberty, killed three men, proclaimed a general emancipation, held the ground for more than thirty hours, were subsequently overpowered and nearly all killed, wounded or captured, ..."

The people of Harper's Ferry, Douglass went on, were outraged by this invasion of their peaceful town in the dead of night, and by the shedding of blood. If we view the raid by itself, apart from the times that gave rise to it, then "it takes rank with the most cold-blooded and atrocious wrongs ever perpetrated."

But, he pointed out, nothing in this world stands alone; everything is linked with everything else. "Every seed," he said, "bears fruit after its own kind, and nothing is reaped which was not sowed." In all of human affairs "there is a seed time, there is a harvest time, and though ages may intervene, . . . yet the harvest nevertheless will surely come. . . . The bloody harvest of Harper's Ferry was ripened by the heat and moisture of merciless bondage for more than two hundred years. That startling cry of alarm on the banks of the Potomac was but the answering back of the avenging angel to the midnight invasions of Christian slave-traders on the sleeping hamlets of Africa."

Some people, continued Douglass, thought that he, Douglass, had a lot to do with planning Brown's raid. But this was not true; it was an honor which he must decline. Douglass proceeded to give to John Brown the most impressive tribute which, perhaps, it was in his power to do. "His zeal in the cause of my race," he said, "was far greater than mine—it was the burning sun to my taper light—mine was bounded by time, his stretched away to the boundless shores of eternity. I could live for the slave, but he could die for him. . . .

This man loved liberty for all men, and for those most despised and scorned, as well as for those most esteemed and honored. "*

* Appropriately Douglass left the manuscript of this eloquent address to the Trustees of Storer College so that they might publish it and use the proceeds to establish a John Brown professorship.

8

DOUGLASS AND LINCOLN
The Meaning of the Civil War

On Tuesday, October 18, 1859, Frederick Douglass was in Philadelphia's National Hall delivering a lecture on "Self-Made Men" when he received the startling news of Harper's Ferry and John Brown's capture. Friends informed him that letters had been found to implicate him in Brown's plot. They urged him to leave town and seek safety.

Even as Douglass was wondering what to do, a telegraph message arrived from Washington, D.C., ordering the sheriff of Philadelphia to arrest the black leader. Fortunately, John Hurn, the telegraph operator on duty, was an antislavery advocate and an admirer of Douglass. He delayed delivery of the telegram for three hours, during which time Douglass fled the city.

Emotions ran high that October, and Douglass was in very real danger. On the train back to Rochester he picked up the *New York Herald*. The front-page headline read "Gerrit Smith, Joshua Giddings, Fred Douglass and Other Abolitionists and Republicans Implicated." There followed a story that Brown had confessed and given sufficient evidence to warrant Douglass's arrest as an accessory to murder.

Back home Douglass scarcely had time to greet his family and burn some potentially incriminating papers before he fled once more, this time to Canada. Soon after he crossed the border the United States district attorney for western New

York arrived in Rochester to arrest him. So determined was Virginia Governor Henry Wise to seize Douglass that he hired a special detective to work undercover and find the fugitive.

Some people called Douglass a coward because he fled. To refute these charges Douglass explained his actions in a letter sent from Canada on October 31 to the Rochester *Democrat and American*. Here he denied taking any part in the attack on Harper's Ferry. But he refused to condemn Brown's raid and praised the captain as a "noble old hero whose one right hand has shaken the foundation of the American Union, and whose ghost will haunt the bedchambers of all the born and unborn slaveholders of Virginia through all their generations." Any effort to overthrow slavery, he said, however violent, was moral. Soon after, Douglass departed once more for England, a trip he had planned well before Harper's Ferry. On November 12 he sailed from Quebec.

In England Douglass learned of Brown's hanging and read his last written prophecy "that the crimes of this *guilty land* will never be purged away, but with Blood." Warmly welcomed on British soil, Douglass again began a triumphant lecture tour. This was cut short, however, by the tragic news of the death of his youngest daughter, Annie. She had been his favorite child and he made immediate plans to return despite any personal danger. Arriving in Rochester in May of 1860, Douglass found that Harper's Ferry had helped touch off a succession of events that would ultimately lead to Southern secession and Civil War.

Eighteen-sixty was a presidential election year, and politics mirrored the divided nature of American society. When the decade of the 1850s had begun the two major political parties, Whig and Democrat, were both viable national organizations. But the tumultuous events of the fifties made it impossible for the political parties to ignore the issue of slavery. Politics came to reflect the growing divisions between North and South. In the aftermath of the 1854 Kansas-Nebraska Act the Whig party disintegrated and the Republican party emerged. Dedicated to keeping slavery out of territories, this new party had virtually no support outside the North. Then in 1860 the

Democratic party split into Northern and Southern factions, paving the way for the election of Republican Abraham Lincoln as the nation's first president elected exclusively by the votes of people in one section of the country.

Though Lincoln and the Republicans promised not to interfere with slavery in the existing states, nevertheless, soon after Lincoln's election the states of the lower South seceded from the Union and in February 1861 formed the Confederacy. Lincoln was inaugurated on March 4, 1861. Little more than a month later Confederate troops opened fire on Fort Sumter, a newly built federal fort located in the harbor of Charleston, South Carolina. In response to this, on April 15, 1861, Lincoln called for 75,000 troops to suppress the insurrection. War had come. Yet although slavery had caused this conflict, for President Lincoln the aim of the war was not to abolish slavery but simply to preserve the Union.

Frederick Douglass, on the other hand, saw the Civil War from the outset as a struggle between freedom and slavery. The sin of slavery, as he saw it, would now be ended even if Americans were forced to shed their blood. John Brown would be vindicated; blacks would at last take their place as citizens and equals. The front page of *Douglass' Monthly* for May 1861 pictured an American eagle and the U.S. flag above the caption, "Freedom for all, or chains for all." Slavery, wrote Douglass, was now exposed "to the keen knife of liberty." It was the hour for "all the righteous forces of the nation to deal a death-blow to the monster evil of the nineteenth century—*Friends of freedom! be up and doing—now is your time.*"

In that same May issue of his *Monthly* Douglass authored an article "How to End the War." He had two proposals. First the aim of the war should be the abolition of slavery: "freedom to the slave should now be proclaimed from the Capitol, and should be seen above the smoke and fire of every battlefield, waving from every loyal flag." Douglass's second plan was to enlist blacks in the war: "*let the slaves and free colored people be called into service, and formed into a liberating army,* to march into the South and raise the banner of Emancipation among the slaves."

Throughout the war Douglass strove to make these two goals realities. Although frequently frustrated by the cautious policies of President Lincoln, he saw his role and that of other abolitionists as the conscience of the Republican party and the North. He also counted on "the inexorable logic of events" to force upon the country the realization "that the war now being waged in this land is a war for and against slavery." In the long run Douglass would have his way. The war did become a battle for emancipation, and blacks, both free and slave, did ultimately play an important part as active combatants.

At the outset of the war the Lincoln administration refused either to proclaim the war to be against slavery or to enlist blacks into the army. Abraham Lincoln would prove to be the central figure in the drama of the Civil War years. He was a complex and paradoxical man, at once idealistic and skeptical, humble and self-assured, warm and reserved. Nowhere were Lincoln's complexities more clearly revealed than in his attitudes toward slavery and blacks. Lincoln opposed slavery all his adult life. To him it was incompatible with America's democratic mission. In an 1854 speech, for instance, he spoke of slavery as a "monstrous injustice." "I hate it," he added, "because it deprives our republican example of its just influence in the world." And not only did Lincoln detest slavery in the abstract, he also on a number of occasions expressed sincere personal sympathy for the slave.

Yet like the vast majority of whites of his generation, Lincoln was not free from the taint of racism. When pressed by Stephen Douglas in their famous 1858 debates, Lincoln admitted that he believed in the superiority of the white race: "I am not, nor ever have been in favor of bringing about in any way the social and political equality of the white and black races. . . ." Race prejudice tempered Lincoln's antislavery sentiment. For him the best solution to America's racial dilemma would be to ship all the blacks back to Africa or some other place outside the United States.

In addition to his personal beliefs, Lincoln was also influenced on racial matters by political considerations. At the outset of hostilities he feared that any policy of emancipation would prevent a quick end to secession and might drive the loyal slave states of Delaware, Maryland, Kentucky, and Missouri into the Confederacy. An abolition policy, Lincoln also presumed, might lessen support for the war among Northern Democrats and conservative Republicans.

Consequently Lincoln's early wartime policies were anything but encouraging to Frederick Douglass. Northern blacks rushed to offer their services in response to the president's first call for military volunteers. But while taking some blacks as army cooks and laborers, the government refused to enlist them as soldiers. Douglass was furious. "The Negro is the key to the situation," he argued, "the pivot upon which the whole rebellion turns." He reproached the North for fighting "the rebels with only one hand, when they might strike effectively with two. . . . They fought with their soft white hand, while they kept their black iron hand chained and helpless behind him."

Douglass became particularly provoked when in September 1861 Lincoln canceled General John Frémont's order declaring the slaves of Missouri rebels to be free. "Many blunders have been committed by the Government at Washington during this war," editorialized Douglass, "but this, we think, is the hugest of them all." Throughout the summer and fall of 1861 and the winter of 1862 Douglass traveled thousands of miles delivering lectures in an effort to educate the North on the true meaning of the war and the need to proclaim the abolition of slavery as a Union war aim. Time and again he chastised "the doubting, hesitating and vacillating policy of the government in regard to the real difficulty—slavery."

Despite his critical tone, Douglass noticed that Northern audiences were increasingly receptive to his message. Instead of the boos and hisses he had experienced frequently in prewar days, he was now listened to respectfully and even enthusiastically. Clearly people were coming to equate abolitionism with patriotism. In this respect, as Douglass had predicted from the start, the war helped further Northern opposition to slavery.

This growing antislavery sentiment of Northern society was soon reflected in Washington. Gradually but steadily the war for the Union was being transformed into a war for freedom. As battlefield casualties mounted, so, too, did support for abolishing slavery. In Congress, antislavery Republicans such as Senator Charles Sumner of Massachusetts and Representative Thaddeus Stevens of Pennsylvania were gaining in influence. These so-called "radical" Republicans argued against slavery not only on moral but also military grounds. It was slave labor, they noted, that enabled the Confederacy to feed and supply its armies. They were coming to agree with Douglass, who had charged that "the very stomach of this rebellion is the Negro in the form of a slave. Arrest that hoe in the hands of the Negro, and you smite the rebellion in the very seat of its life."

Congress took its first step toward abolition in April of 1862 by passing an act outlawing slavery in the District of Columbia. This was a moderate measure that provided compensation to slaveowners; Lincoln signed it into law. In June 1862 slavery was banned in the territories. Though this act affected few actual slaves, it did fulfill the Republican party's pledge and more importantly established a significant precedent. That July, Congress authorized the government to confiscate the slaves of masters who supported the Confederacy.

Finally in late September 1862, President Lincoln, responding to growing political pressures, foreign policy considerations, and recent military success, pledged that on January 1, 1863, he would issue an emancipation proclamation freeing all the slaves in states still in rebellion. This proposed proclamation neither applied to loyal slave states nor to occupied areas; in effect it only offered freedom to those slaves in states where the national government did not yet have control. Nevertheless, antislavery advocates looked forward to New Year's Day with great anticipation. At last the Union would be committed to the abolition of slavery as a central purpose of the war.

On January 1, 1863, Douglass took part in a vigil at Tremont Temple in Boston. Several thousand black and white abolitionists listened to Douglass and other speakers while awaiting word that emancipation had come. The wait for what Douglass termed that "bolt from the sky, which should rend the fetters of four millions of slaves" was long in coming. Not until ten that evening did a messenger burst into the crowded hall to exclaim: "It is coming! It is on the wires!" Shouts, prayers, cheers, and tears of joy filled the temple. Soon thousands of voices united in the spiritual, "Sound the loud timbrel [tambourine] o'er Egypt's dark sea, Jehovah hath triumphed, his people are free." Celebrations continued through the night.

Though Douglass saw clearly the limitations of Lincoln's Emancipation Proclamation, he interpreted it, in his words, as "more than it purported, and saw in its spirit a life and power far beyond its letter. Its meaning to me was the entire abolition of slavery, wherever the evil could be reached by the federal arm, and I saw that its moral power would extend much further." What had begun as the desperate and despised crusade of a small band of dedicated abolitionists fighting for freedom against overwhelming odds suddenly seemed within reach. The war, Douglass declared, was finally "invested with sanctity."

In addition to proclaiming slaves in Confederate states free, the Emancipation Proclamation also announced that black recruits would be accepted into the armed services of the United States "to garrison forts . . . and other places, and to man vessels of all sorts. . . ." In Lincoln's mind, evidently, blacks were not to have the honor of fighting for their freedom as soldiers; the United States would recruit them only as fortress workers, or as stevedores and deck hands in the naval service. Nonetheless, the fulfillment of Douglass's ideal of freeing the slaves and having them fight for freedom seemed close at hand. Governor John Andrew of Massachusetts, an abolitionist, had previously petitioned the War Department for permission to raise black troops. In late January 1863 he received official authorization and announced the formation of the first Northern black unit, the Massachusetts 54th Regiment. Since the black population of Massachusetts was small, Governor Andrew soon called upon Douglass and other black leaders to help with recruiting throughout the Northern states.

Through the late winter and spring of 1863 Douglass devoted himself to black recruitment. He traveled widely urging blacks to "fly to arms, and smite with death the power that would bury the government and your liberty in the same hopeless grave." He also authored a famous article, "Men of Color, to Arms." This was first published in the March 1863 edition of his *Monthly*, then reprinted in numerous newspapers and later issued as a broadside. In ringing, poetic language Douglass appealed to black pride, patriotism, courage, honor, and duty:

> The day dawns; the morning star is bright upon the horizon! The iron gate of our prison stands half open. One gallant rush from the North will fling it wide open, while four millions of our brothers and sisters shall march out into liberty. The chance is now given you to end in a day the bondage of centuries, and to rise in one bound from social degradation to the plane of common equality with all other varieties of men. Remember Denmark Vesey of Charleston; remember Nathaniel Turner of Southampton; remember Shields Green and Copeland, who followed John Brown, and fell as glorious martyrs for the cause of the slave.

It was as if Douglass wished to see his fight with the slave breaker Covey replicated a thousandfold. Black manhood would assert itself. "Liberty won by white men," he charged, "would lose half its luster. Who would be free themselves must strike the blow. Better even die free, than to live like slaves."

Douglass personally succeeded in enlisting two companies of black soldiers, including his sons Charles and Lewis. On

May 28, 1863, he was in Boston proudly watching the ceremonies when the Massachusetts 54th Regiment, including his recruits, marched through the streets and embarked from Boston Harbor for the war in the South.

Negro recruitment was extremely important for Douglass. Only through black participation in the war, he believed, could abolition and full citizenship for Negroes be established: "Once let the black man get upon his person the brass letters U.S.; let him get an eagle on his button, and a musket on his shoulder, and bullets in his pocket, and there is no power on earth . . . which can deny that he has earned the right of citizenship in the United States."

Yet while Douglass met with success in his recruitment efforts, he and other blacks soon realized that Negro troops were not being treated equally. Not only were they placed in segregated units under the supervision of white officers, but they also received less pay than white soldiers of similar rank. Even worse, it soon became evident that the Confederacy refused to treat black soldiers by the ordinary conventions of war. Captured blacks routinely were being killed or sold into slavery rather than imprisoned. Such atrocities were common knowledge, yet no official protest came from Washington.

Douglass protested. In late July of 1863 he obtained an audience with President Lincoln to voice the grievances of black soldiers. Though of different races and very different backgrounds, Douglass and Lincoln had much in common. Both began life in humble circumstances and in their rise to prominance epitomized the American ideal of the self-made man. Both men also were viewed as representatives of their respective races and because of this role both tried to lead exemplary lives. Just as Lincoln's rise from log cabin to White House symbolized the great distance a white man could travel, so, too, did Frederick Douglass's audience with the president symbolize the great advance a black man could make from servitude to public celebrity.

Douglass's attitude toward the president had changed markedly since the Emancipation Proclamation and the enlistment of black troops. Douglass had no illusions. He realized the rapid wartime gains for blacks were largely the result of the quarrel between two warring groups of white Americans. But he was now willing to ally with the administration in order to assure the recognition of the Negroes' claims on the nation.

When Douglass entered Lincoln's White House office in late July 1863 he found the president seated in a low armchair, his feet outstretched. Lincoln's lined face showed signs of strain and fatigue. But on hearing Douglass announced, the president rose and cordially shook the black leader's hand. Douglass tried to introduce himself but was cut short by Lincoln who said similingly: "I know who you are, Mr. Douglass. . . . Sit down. I am glad to see you."

Their conversation quickly turned to the purpose of the visit. Douglass urged the president to grant black soldiers equal pay, to give captured black troops who were murdered or mistreated government protection through a policy of retaliation, and to allow meritorious black soldiers a chance for promotion, including the granting of commissions.

Lincoln's answers were frank but disappointing. He told Douglass that to give black soldiers equal pay with whites would run counter to popular feeling, though he did promise "that in the end they shall have the same pay as white soldiers." He assured Douglass that he deplored the Confederate treatment of captured blacks, but balked at any retaliatory action. On Douglass's last point about black promotions, however, Lincoln pledged "to sign any commission to colored soldiers whom his Secretary of War commended."

Douglass left the White House greatly moved by Lincoln's honesty and candor, even though the president's answers did not entirely please the black man. Lincoln for his part seems to have been both impressed and influenced by Douglass. On July 30, only days after their meeting, the president did order that retaliatory measures be taken for every Union prisoner killed or sold into slavery in violation of the rules of war. Before the war ended most black soldiers were receiving equal pay and some at least the chance for promotion. All told, during the last two years of the war nearly 200,000 African-Americans served in the Union armies, and when given the chance to fight proved as brave as anyone. More than 30,000 blacks died fighting for freedom and the Union.

After leaving Lincoln's office, Douglass met with Secretary of War Edwin Stanton to argue his cause further. In the midst of defending his department's treatment of black troops, Stanton surprised Douglass with an offer of a commission if he would aid in the recruitment of black soldiers in the lower Mississippi Valley. Pleased by both the opportunity to become the first black military officer and to further the range of his recruiting activities, Douglass accepted.

Returning to Rochester, he began making preparations for his new job. This was the appropriate time, he decided, to close his paper. On August 16, 1863, the last issue of *Douglass' Monthly* appeared, ending for Douglass 16 years of successful editing and publishing. His affairs in order, he now waited to go. But the promised commission never came. He received a letter ordering him to report to General Lorenzo Thomas in Vicksburg, and, in response to his note of inquiry, a second letter stating his salary, but no commission.

Embittered by this experience, Douglass refused to report to Vicksburg. Instead he again took to the lecture platform and once more assumed the role of critic of the administration and the abolitionists alike. In the aftermath of emancipation many white abolitionists acted as if their work was done. At the annual meeting of the American Anti-Slavery Society in December 1863 most of the speeches recalled past activities and were self-congratulatory. When Douglass took the platform he reminded the delegates "that our work will not be done until the colored man is admitted a full member in good and regular standing in the American body politic." Not only must slavery be abolished, but color prejudice in the North as well. Blacks must be given full citizenship, including the ballot. "There never was a time," he concluded, "when anti-slavery work was more needed than now."

Douglass developed his analysis of the meaning of the Civil War into a thoughtful and moving oration titled "The Mission of the War." During the winter and spring of 1864 he delivered this 90-minute speech throughout the North. In a letter that February Douglass wrote: "I am this winter doing more with my voice than with my pen. I am heard with more than usual attention and hope I am doing some good in my day and generation."

The speech warned of the dangers of war weariness that might incline the North to accept a peace that did not complete the work of abolition. "It is true," he stated, "that the war seems long. But this very slow progress is an essential element of its effectiveness. Like the slow convalescence of some patients the fault is less chargeable to the medicine than to the deep-seated character of the disease." This war was not being fought for the restoration of the old Union. That Union was diseased with slavery and prejudice. Douglass described his vision of the nation: "What we now want is a country—a free country—a country not saddened by the footprints of a single slave—and nowhere cursed by the presence of a slaveholder. We want a country which shall not brand the Declaration of Independence as a lie." It would be a country where "the New England schoolhouse is bound to take the place of the Southern whipping-post. . . .

A country in which no man shall be fined for reading a book or imprisoned for selling a book . . . where no man may be imprisoned or flogged or sold for learning to read, or teaching a fellow mortal how to read." Without the creation of such a nation dedicated to liberty and justice for all the war would be "little better than a gigantic enterprise for shedding human blood."

As the war dragged on through the spring and summer of 1864 Douglass's warnings about the effects of war weariness on the North seemed to be borne out. Democrats and even some Republicans clamored for peace at any price. In late August, fearing he might be pressured to conclude such a peace before slavery was completely abolished, President Lincoln summoned Douglass to the White House. He proposed to him a scheme not unlike that which John Brown had first revealed to Douglass in 1847. Lincoln's plan was to have Douglass and other blacks go into the South behind enemy lines to spread the word of emancipation and help lead as many slaves to freedom as possible before the war ended. Douglass agreed to help in this scheme and began making plans. However the fall of Atlanta on September 2 and other Union military successes quickly put an end to the peace-at-any-price sentiment.

Northern victories also strengthened Lincoln's chances for re-election that November. Though Douglass earlier had given his support to the third-party candidacy of radical Republican John Frémont, after his August meeting with Lincoln he backed the president. No doubt he was flattered by Lincoln's consulting him; but it was the Democratic party's nomination of George McClellan on a peace platform that fully convinced Douglass of the need to stick with Lincoln.

Early in October 1864 Douglass attended the national convention of colored men in Syracuse, the first such convention in a decade. Elected president of the convention, Douglass helped draft its "Address to the People of the United States." Though this document called for Negro suffrage and other rights in advance of what Lincoln appeared willing to grant, nevertheless, the convention came out in support of Lincoln. For Douglass and many blacks this marked the beginning of a life-long commitment to the Republican party.

Pleased at Lincoln's reelection, Douglass was present in Washington for the second inaugural in March 1865. By this time the collapse of the Confederacy was imminent. Already Douglass had been able to travel through Virginia and to deliver six lectures in Baltimore—a triumphant homecoming for the former slave who was now an internationally famous free man. When guards attempted to prevent Douglass from attending Lincoln's gala inaugural celebration the president intervened on his behalf, after which they chatted cordially. This was to be the last time these two leaders would meet.

Douglass had just returned to Rochester on April 14, 1865, when he heard the news of Lincoln's assassination. That evening Douglass delivered a eulogy to the slain president. His speech paid tribute to the martyred leader and referred to the assassination as "the crowning crime of slavery."

Before their August 1864 meeting Lincoln had said to the Reverend John Eaton that he considered Douglass "one of the most meritorious men, if not the most meritorious man in the United States." Lincoln had spoken with his wife about his wish to give the black leader some token of his regard. Soon after the assassination, Mrs. Lincoln sent the president's favorite walking stick to Douglass. This would remain one of Douglass's most cherished mementos.

Yet Douglass was ambivalent about Lincoln. Personally he liked and admired him. "In all my interviews with Mr. Lincoln," Douglass later recalled, "I was impressed with his entire freedom from popular prejudice against the colored race." Not surprisingly Douglass sympathized with Lincoln's humble background and saw this as a source of his strength: "The hard condition of his early life, which would have depressed and broken down weaker men, only gave greater life, vigor, and buoyancy to the heroic spirit of Abraham Lincoln." But Douglass fully knew that what Lincoln accomplished in ending slavery had been done slowly, calculatingly, and reluctantly.

On April 14, 1876, eleven years to the day after Lincoln's death, Douglass delivered an "Oration in Memory of Abraham Lincoln" before an audience consisting of President Ulysses S. Grant, government officials, and a large number of blacks. The occasion was the unveiling of a bronze statue in honor of the slain President. The money for this statue had been raised by blacks. Douglass began by reminding the black members of his audience that "Abraham Lincoln was not, in the fullest sense of the word, either our man or our model. . . . He was preeminently the white man's President entirely devoted to the welfare of white men. He was ready and willing at any time during the first years of his administration to deny, postpone, and sacrifice the rights of humanity in the colored people to promote the welfare or the white people of this country." Throughout the war the faith of blacks "was often taxed and strained to the uttermost" as Lincoln "tarried long in the mountain."

Yet despite these reservations, Douglass in reevaluating the president claimed that he had been truly worthy of the Negro's faith: "Though the Union was more to him than our freedom or our future, under his wise and beneficent rule we saw ourselves gradually lifted from the depths of slavery to the heights of liberty and manhood." Douglass concluded that "the hour and the man of our redemption had somehow met in the person of Abraham Lincoln." Providence, he believed, had used Lincoln as the primary agent of black freedom.

By the time of Douglass's eulogy the myth of Lincoln as the Great Emancipator was well established. No doubt Douglass realized that by identifying Lincoln with the cause of racial justice and equality the memory of the martyred president could be used to further those goals. It is not surprising therefore that Frederick Douglass helped create and perpetuate the Lincoln myth.

9

DOUGLASS
AND THE RECONSTRUCTION
OF THE NATION

T he Civil War was over in April 1865, and by the end of that year the Thirteenth Amendment was ratified, forever abolishing slavery. Douglass's greatest goal was accomplished; his joy was boundless. And yet, as he later recalled, "a strange and, perhaps, perverse feeling came over me." His happiness over the great historic events that had transformed America "was slightly tinged with a feeling of sadness." Having devoted most of his adult years to the cause of abolition he now felt he had reached the end of the noblest and best part of his life: "my school was broken up, my church disbanded, and the beloved congregation dispersed, never to come together again. The antislavery platform had performed its work, and my voice was no longer needed."

Now 47 years old, his once dark hair turning white, his still robust frame some pounds heavier, Douglass pondered his future: "where should I go, and what should I do?" He had a few thousand dollars saved from his lectures and the sales of his second autobiography, *My Bondage and My Freedom* (1855). With this he thought he might buy a farm "and earn an honest living by tilling the soil." His children were now grown and married and he hoped able to take care of themselves.

Yet however tempted Douglass may have been to retire from public life after 25 years of struggle in the cause of freedom, he fully realized "that the Negro still had a cause, and that he needed my voice and pen, with others, to plead for it." For another 30 years, until his death in 1895, Douglass would pursue his career as orator, journalist, reformer, author, politician, diplomat, and black leader. But in some ways his best years *were* behind him. In the prewar period, he had stood outside the political power structure. Rejected both because he was black and a radical abolitionist, he had been stimulated by the struggle and had emerged as a major voice of dissent. But in postwar America Douglass was a celebrity, and as a loyal Republican and office-seeker he generally chose to function within the existing party system. From such a position he would play new roles, some with great eminence, some without. But he was often forced to temper his moral idealism and to learn the art of political compromise. Unfortunately he was to see his vision of freedom born of emancipation undermined by the harsh realities of continuing white racism.

Douglass had worked hard to make the Civil War a struggle for abolition. Soon after Lee's surrender at Appomatox, he set out to ensure that the reunification of the nation would not take place at the expense of black Americans. One of his first tasks was to rally other abolitionists to continue the fight for black rights. At the May 1865 meeting of the American Anti-Slavery Society William Lloyd Garrison introduced a resolution calling for the dissolution of the organization. He declared his faith that the North in reconstructing the defeated Confederacy would insist on "guarantees for the protection of the freedmen." The Anti-Slavery society, he concluded, was no longer "of special importance."

Frederick Douglass took the lead in opposing this position. "The work of the American Anti-Slavery Society will not have been completed," he proclaimed, "until the black men of the South, and the black men of the North, shall have been admitted, fully and completely, into the body politic of

America." With the strong support of Wendell Phillips, Douglass convinced the delegates by more than a two to one margin to reject Garrison's resolution. With this defeat, Garrison retired from the organization and later that year closed *The Liberator.*

The key need for black Americans, according to Douglass, was the ballot: "without the elective franchise the Negro will still be practically a slave. Individual ownership has been abolished; but if we restore the Southern States without this measure, we shall establish an ownership of the blacks by the community among which they live." Lincoln in life had advocated a lenient policy for readmitting rebel states and had shown only slight interest in black voting rights. Nevertheless, Douglass praised the martyred president as one who if still alive would be in the forefront of the struggle for full citizenship and the vote for black people.

Douglass was particularly upset by the policies of Lincoln's successor, Andrew Johnson. Johnson, a Tennessee Democrat and former slaveholder, favored a quick restoration of the Union with no protection for freed slaves beyond the prohibition of slavery. With Congress in recess during the summer and fall of 1865 new state governments were reconstructed throughout the South. Though Johnson attempted to restrict the participation of former Confederate leaders and wealthy planters, in state after state such men regained positions of power. These newly constituted states also passed a series of vagrancy and apprenticeship laws severely restricting the civil and economic rights of ex-slaves. These so called "Black Codes" virtually reconstituted slavery in everything but name. In Mississippi, for instance, blacks were denied the right to purchase or even rent land. In South Carolina they needed a special license to hold any job except that of field hand. Most state codes denied blacks the right to purchase or carry firearms, or to assemble after dark. Any black determined to be "idle" could be arrested and put to work on a state chain gang, or auctioned off to a planter and forced to work without pay for as long as a year. Despite this, by the time Congress reconvened in early December 1865, President Johnson declared the Union to be restored.

To Douglass, Johnson's policy of reconstruction meant the abandonment of the former slaves to the old master class. In a January 1866 speech he referred to presidential policy as "the crime of crimes." It was "nothing less than the base and wanton betrayal by a triumphant nation of their only allies and friends. . . ." He denounced the President as "a traitor to the cause of freedom."

On February 7, 1866, Douglass headed a delegation of blacks who called on Johnson at the White House. They urged him to grant Negroes the vote. Douglass attempted to pressure the president by reference to the commitments of Lincoln. "Your noble and humane predecessor," he said, "placed in our hands the sword to assist in saving the nation and we do hope that you, his able successor, will favorably regard the placing in our hands the ballot with which to save ourselves."

In his reply Johnson claimed to be a friend of the black race. "If I know myself, and the feelings of my own heart, they have been for the colored man. I have owned slaves and bought slaves, but I never sold one." He went so far as to declare himself the Negroes' "Moses" who would lead blacks "from bondage to freedom." He claimed to oppose Negro suffrage for the sake of the freedmen. Giving blacks the ballot, he insisted, would only lead to race war. Besides, he argued, it was up to the individual states and not the national government to decide who should vote. Colonization, he concluded, would be the best option for the former slaves.

Angered by Johnson's remarks, Douglass tried to reply only to be cut short by the president, who quickly ushered the black visitors out of his office. Enraged at this, Douglass later that day attempted to refute Johnson's arguments in an open letter published in the *Washington Chronicle.* Johnson's policies, Douglass stated, were "unsound and prejudicial" to both Negroes and the nation as a whole. He denied that black suffrage would cause a race war between Negroes and poor whites. Such hostility was the product of slavery, not freedom. "Peace between races is not to be secured by degrading one race and exalting another," Douglass wrote, "but by maintaining a state of equal justice between all classes." As for colonization, Douglass argued that the removal of black Americans would cause a terrible shock to the nation's "prosperity and peace." Only enemies of the United States, he concluded, "would argue that Negroes could be tolerated . . . in a state of the most degrading slavery and oppression, and must be cast away driven into exile, for . . . having been freed from their chains."

Douglass's open letter was widely reprinted. The Republican press, already critical of Johnson's policies, used the interview and Douglass's reply to further attack the president. The abolitionists were outraged at Johnson's blatant racial prejudice. Elizabeth Cady Stanton noted "how much better Douglass understands the philosophy of social life and republican institutions than the President." The *Anti-Slavery Standard* called Johnson's speech "brutal and insolent" and wrote that if he represented the best of his race "we blush for the white race. Dignity, force of speech, modesty, manliness, simple faith in justice, weight of character, are all on the side of the Negro." The president for his part assumed he had gotten the better of the exchange. In private he remarked to his secretary: "I know that damned Douglass; he's just like any nigger, and he would sooner cut a white man's throat as not."

But Douglass and other blacks were not alone in opposing presidential policies. When the Republican-dominated Congress met in December 1865 it rejected Johnson's plan of reconstruction and refused to seat the representatives from the seceded Southern states. Congress created a joint committee to oversee Reconstruction. Dominated by such radical Republicans as Charles Sumner and Thaddeus Stevens, Congress now sought a reconstruction policy that would limit the political role of ex-Confederates and provide some protection for freedmen. Though only a few of the radicals truly believed in racial equality, most were convinced that blacks should have the same basic rights as other citizens. They were also aware of the political advantages of granting blacks the ballot since it was assumed that newly enfranchised Negro voters would support the party of emancipation.

Soon after Douglass and the black delegation met with Johnson, relations between the president and Congress became tense. Johnson vetoed two bills that had passed with overwhelming Republican support. The first, the Freedmen's Bureau bill, aimed to extend the life of the agency charged with providing former slaves with relief and assistance. The second, a civil rights bill, was intended to guarantee black citizenship and nullify the Black Codes. By early summer 1866 Congress repassed both bills with the necessary two-thirds support to override the president's veto. As a further guarantee of Negro citizenship, Congress in June passed the Fourteenth Amendment and sent it to the states for ratification. This important amendment gave the federal government responsibility for guaranteeing equal rights under the law to all Americans. States were expressly prohibited from depriving any person of "life, liberty, or property, without due process of law" and from denying "equal protection of the laws." With Johnson's urging, all the Southern states except Tennessee rejected the amendment.

President Johnson tried to unite behind him conservative Republicans and the Democratic party in opposition to the radical Republican-controlled Congress. He looked forward to the 1866 congressional elections as a chance for the voters to choose between his reconstruction policy or Congress's. To get his message to the voters Johnson arranged a National Union convention to publicize his program. Meeting in Philadelphia in mid-August, delegates denounced congressional reconstruction as "unjust and revolutionary." They praised the president and appealed to the people to elect congressmen who would support his policies.

Not to be outdone, radical Republicans called their own convention of loyal Southern Unionists also to meet in Philadelphia in September. Though primarily a gathering of Southern Republicans, Northern representatives were invited as honorary delegates. Included among the Northern Republican delegates was Frederick Douglass, who had been elected by his fellow party members from Rochester. Even before arriving in Philadelphia, however, his selection proved controversial. On the train to the meeting a group of delegates urged him not to participate. His presence, they argued, would weaken Republican chances in the upcoming elections. Douglass refused to listen. Not to attend the convention, he told his fellow delegates, "would contradict the principle and practice of my life."

On the morning of September 3, several hundred delegates met for a grand procession. They were to march two abreast through the streets of Philadelphia from Independence Hall to National Hall where the meetings were to be held. As the lines formed it became clear that the delegates were avoiding the black leader. Just when it appeared that Douglass would be forced to march alone, Theodore Tilton, a friend and editor of the radical New York *Independent,* came and took Douglass's arm. To his pleasure Douglass found that "along the whole line of march my presence was cheered repeatedly and enthusiastically."

At the convention itself Douglass played a conspicuous part in gaining support for Negro suffrage. After three days of separate meetings of Southern and Northern delegates, Douglass, Tilton, and Anna Dickinson, a young Quaker feminist and abolitionist, made a plea to the Southern Unionists to back black voting rights. Douglass, who in his words, "looked upon suffrage to the Negro as the only measure which would prevent him from being thrust back into slavery," delivered a magnificent speech. Though some border state delegates bolted the convention, the overwhelming majority of Southern delegates supported the extension of suffrage to blacks and offered public thanks to Douglass and Dickinson. The Fifteenth Amendment granting blacks the vote would not pass for four more years. But the Philadelphia meeting can be seen as the starting point of that amendment. Before the convention black suffrage was largely an issue brought forth by isolated individuals like Douglass. From that time forward the question of enfranchising the Negro became a public issue increasingly supported by the Republican party and much of the public.

Following the two Philadelphia conventions the fall election campaign became heated. Johnson went on an extended speaking tour, denouncing his opponents as "blood-suckers," and comparing himself to Christ. But if the election was a referendum on the conflicting reconstruction policies of the president and congressional Republicans, the verdict was clear. Nearly everywhere Johnson supporters went down to defeat. Republicans won a three-to-one majority in Congress. Even moderate Republicans interpreted the elections as a clear call for the reconstruction, rather than mere restoration, of the South. Republican radicals, therefore, were now free to reconstruct the South as they saw fit.

The new Congress placed the Confederacy under martial law and divided the South into five military districts. Each state was required to hold new constitutional conventions with delegates chosen by universal manhood suffrage, excepting ex-Confederate leaders. For readmission into the Union it was required that each new state constitution guarantee black suffrage. In addition, each Southern state was required to ratify the Fourteenth Amendment before submitting the new constitution to Congress for approval.

Douglass thoroughly supported radical Republican efforts to remake the South. To him Reconstruction was a continuation of the war against the traitorous Slave Power. He saw it as a "great work of national regeneration and entire purification." Two things, however, made him uneasy.

First, he still saw a need for a constitutional amendment guaranteeing Negro suffrage. Though Congress was enforcing equal political rights for black males in the Southern states, once these states had been readmitted to the Union ways might be found to deprive blacks of the vote. Another reason Douglass desired an amendment enfranchising blacks was the North. Republicans had taken no steps to deal with racism and the denial of rights to black people in the Northern states. New Jersey, Connecticut, Pennsylvania, and most western states prohibited blacks from voting. Even Douglass's home state of New York imposed high property qualifications on black voters. A constitutional amendment, therefore, was necessary to advance political equality not only in the South but throughout the nation.

The second problem Douglass found with radical Reconstruction was that the Republicans had put forward no land policy. "The Negro must have a right to the land," he proclaimed. Without land the freedmen would remain dependent on the former slaveowners. Charles Sumner, Thaddeus Stevens, and several other radicals in Congress favored land redistribution. However, although small experiments in resettling blacks on confiscated lands had been made during and just after the war, President Johnson ended all such programs. Granting blacks citizenship and voting rights had strong support among Northern whites in the years after the war. But giving blacks land ran counter to Americans' basic beliefs in individualism and the sanctity of private property. As the New York Times editorialized, any "attempt to justify the confiscation of southern land under the pretence of doing justice to the freedmen strikes at the root of all property rights in both sections."

Douglass, too, opposed confiscation as a means of land redistribution. A firm believer in self-reliance and the traditional values of hard work, sobriety, and thrift, he had difficulty justifying any scheme that violated this individualistic code. Douglass saw himself as a model of the self-made man. He had been able to succeed in life despite the obstacles of slavery and racism; he assumed other blacks could do the same. He never tired of preaching self-reliance.

These beliefs moderated Douglass's radicalism and made him less able to recognize the unbelievable economic handicaps confronting America's 4 million former slaves. Instead of confiscation and redistribution of Southern lands, Douglass urged only that blacks be given federal assistance to help them purchase land. Specifically he called for a National Land and Loan Company empowered to buy large tracts of Southern land and to sell small farms to the freedmen on easy terms. Even this moderate proposal, however, failed to muster sufficient support to become public policy. In the long run the failure to give the freed slaves any of the land they had worked proved to be the greatest shortcoming of radical Reconstruction and the key to its failure.

Reflecting on the rejection of land redistribution in 1880, Douglass stated: "Could the nation have been induced to listen to those stalwart Republicans, Thaddeus Stevens and Charles Sumner, some of the evils which we now suffer would have been averted. The Negro would not today be on his knees, as he is, supplicating the old master class to give him leave to toil. . . . He would not now be swindled out of his hard earnings by money orders for wages with no money in them . . . as is now the case because left by our emancipation measures at the mercy of the men who had robbed him all his life and his people for centuries." Douglass knew well the hardships facing the freedmen in the immediate aftermath of the war. Not only had he himself been a slave, he also toured areas of the South after the war where he witnessed the plight of impoverished landless blacks.

In the summer of 1867 the devastating human effects of slavery were made personally vivid to him when he met his brother, Perry, for the first time in 40 years. Perry had spent more than half a century in slavery, most of it in the Deep South. After the war he made contact with Douglass and through intermediaries was sent to Rochester with his wife and four children. "The meeting of my brother after nearly forty years of separation," wrote Douglass, "is an event altogether too affecting for words to describe." Douglass quickly set about having a small house built for Perry and his family next to his own home.

Douglass was overjoyed at this reunion, but disturbed too. The contrast between his exceptional life and that of his "old slavery-scarred and long-lost brother" could not have been greater. Writing to his friend Tilton, Douglass noted that Perry was so different from him it was "as if he had lived on another planet." Seeing his uneducated brother "deeply marked by the hardships and sorrows of that hateful condition" forced Douglass once again to recognize the degrading legacy of slavery. "If slavery were not dead, and I did not in some sort wish to forget its terrible hardships, blighting curses, and shocking horrors, I would try to write a narrative of my brother Perry's bondage."

That same summer of 1867 in which Perry and his family came to Rochester, President Johnson unexpectedly offered to appoint Douglass as head of the Freedman's Bureau. This was the major government agency to assist former slaves. Its budget that year was nearly $7 million; some 2,000 men were in its employ. For a black man to head such an agency would be a great honor. Douglass was certainly tempted. However, he realized the offer was a political ploy and that he would have no real support from the president. He also did not wish to be under any obligation to Johnson. When Douglass's refusal became public that September, Tilton applauded that "the greatest black man in the nation did not become a tool of the meanest white."

The wisdom of Douglass's decision soon became evident. Johnson's continued efforts to undermine congressional Reconstruction increasingly lost him support and in 1868 brought him within one vote of losing his office through impeachment. Though acquitted, Johnson was thoroughly discredited. Eager to gain control of the White House, the Republican party in May of 1868 nominated the Civil War hero General Ulysses S. Grant.

Douglass supported Grant and threw himself vigorously into the campaign. In an oft-repeated speech, "The Work Before Us," he denounced the Democrats as the party of treason. The election, he argued, was "but a continuation of the mighty struggle of a great nation to shake off an old and worn-out system of barbarism. . . . It is a part of our thirty years' effort to place the country in harmony with the age. . . ."

Douglass's campaigning helped bring out more than 700,000 black voters, most of whom supported the Republican candidate. Since Grant won by a popular majority of only slightly more than 300,000, the message was clear:

the black vote had been decisive. For years Douglass had been arguing that black suffrage was a matter of right and justice. Now Republicans saw it as a matter of practical necessity. In February 1869 the Fifteenth Amendment granting blacks the vote received the necessary two-thirds majority in both houses of Congress and was submitted to the states for ratification. On March 30, 1870, President Grant proclaimed the suffrage amendment adopted.

Celebrations were the order of the day. Not since the Emancipation Proclamation had there been such rejoicing among blacks and abolitionists. On April 19, 1870, the American Anti-Slavery Society met for the last time. Its goals seemed fulfilled. Speaking before the jubilant gathering of old friends, Douglass told of his amazement at the momentous changes that had occurred over the last decade: "I seem to myself to be living in a new world. The sun does not shine as it used to. . . . Not only the slave emancipated, but a personal liberty bill, a civil rights bill, admitted to give testimony in courts of justice, given the right to vote, eligible not only to Congress, but the Presidential chair—and all for a class stigmatized but a little while ago as worthless goods and chattels. . . ."

A new era seemed to be dawning. Douglass could now proudly proclaim his Americanism, his pride in "our country." "We are all together now," he declared. "We are fellow-citizens of a common country. What a country—fortunate in its institutions, in its fifteenth amendment, in its future."

More than a month of celebrations of the Fifteenth Amendment's ratification culminated in a giant mid-May ceremony in Baltimore. Accompanied by brass bands, some 20,000 blacks and whites marched in a parade to Monument Square. After a number of speeches and more band music Douglass came forward to address the crowd. He reminisced about his youthful experiences in Baltimore as a slave and thanked God he was now in that same city celebrating the achievement of voting rights for his people. "We have a future," he shouted in conclusion; "everything is possible to us."

As the day-long festivities drew to a close, the chairman rose to read a series of resolutions expressing thanks to God, to the Republican party, and to President Grant. Each proclamation was adopted with loud acclaim. But the greatest applause came in response to the last resolution, recognizing Douglass as "the foremost man of color in the times" and appealing to him "by the power of his magnificent manhood" to lead blacks "to a higher, broader, and nobler manhood."

10

REPUBLICAN OFFICEHOLDER

The Civil War and Reconstruction had given Douglass the vision of a society in which social advancement would be open to all on the basis of merit, not race or class. For blacks it was to be the fulfillment of the age-old American dream. Much had been accomplished. The Thirteenth, Fourteenth, and Fifteenth Amendments had given blacks freedom, citizenship, and the vote. In the reconstructed Southern states real progress had been made in establishing public school systems, rebuilding war-torn economies, and in attempting to create a truly interracial political democracy.

But Douglass's dream of "a New Era" was not to be. Since land was not given to the ex-slaves most of them continued to be dependent on white landowners. The vast majority of Southern blacks remained propertyless and poor. Even the political rights of the freedmen were to prove short-lived. Throughout the South the remnants of the white patrols of slavery days reconstituted themselves as secret white societies such as the Ku Klux Klan. These organizations terrorized blacks who attempted to vote or hold office. Violence, intimidation, and economic coercion increasingly made a mockery of black freedom and undermined Republican control of the South. In state after state white supremacy reasserted itself.

Had the Republican-dominated national government been more active in its efforts to enforce equal rights for blacks the results of Reconstruction might have been more positive. But by the 1870s Northern moral idealism was waning, while racial prejudice was on the rise. More and more the government acquiesced as white supremacists "redeemed" Southern state governments and systematically disenfranchised the freedmen. The radical Republican champions of black rights, Stevens and Sumner, died in 1868 and 1874, respectively. The new generation of Republicans coming to power were more concerned with other issues than racial equality. The final end of Reconstruction came in 1877 when the last federal troops were withdrawn from the South and the federal presence there was terminated.

Douglass was deeply discouraged. He realized that black freedom "has been more in name than in fact." Speaking in 1875 he noted that "the world has never seen any people turned loose to such destitution as were the four million slaves of the South. . . . They were free! free to hunger; . . . free to the pitiless wrath of enraged masters, who, since they could no longer control them, were willing to see them starve. They were free, without roofs to cover them, or bread to eat, or land to cultivate."

Although dejected, Douglass did not give in to despair. He was sure that the battle "for the ultimate peace and freedom of my race" would one day be won. Somewhat naively he placed his faith in the Republican party. To Douglass American politics was not a contest between two legitimate political parties representing diverse factions and constituencies. Instead he saw politics as an ongoing struggle between the forces of good and evil. "There are but two real parties in the country," he claimed. "One is the party loyal to liberty, justice, and good order, and the other is the party in sympathy with the defeated rebellion." He repeatedly attacked the Democrats as the "party of murder, robbery, treason, dishonesty, and fraud." The Republicans in contrast had "saved the nation, conquered the rebellion, put down the slaveholders' war, and liberated four millions of bondmen."

In addition to seeing support for the Republican party as the only available way to advance his race, Douglass also hoped his dedication to that party would result in his own political preferment. As a loyal Republican and the nation's foremost black spokesperson he desired and expected to be given a political job. For his campaign services in Grant's 1868 election Douglass hoped to get the Rochester postmastership; but he was disappointed.

In January of 1871, however, President Grant did give Douglass an appointment. At the time the administration was looking into the possibility of seizing Santo Domingo (now the Dominican Republic) as part of its aggressive ambitions in the Caribbean. A commission was set up to inquire into this matter and Douglass was named as an assistant secretary. He accompanied the commission to the country, but found his duties to be minimal. He supported the commission's recommendation for annexation believing this to be part of America's "mission." But this was later blocked in the Senate.

Two incidents marred Douglass's service on the commission. On the return voyage he was barred from the dining room of the government-owned vessel. Informed of the incident, President Grant did nothing to reprimand those responsible. Soon after the commission returned to Washington its members were invited to dine at the White House. Douglass was left out. In prewar days he would have vehemently protested such racist insults. Now he accepted these humiliations in silence.

In 1872 Douglass again worked for Grant's presidential candidacy. "If as a class we are slighted by the Republican party," he told an all black audience, "we are as a class murdered by the Democratic party." Ironically, while campaigning for Grant, Douglass, without being consulted, became the first black nominated for the vice presidency. He was chosen by the Equal Rights party on a ticket headed by Victoria Woodhull, a noted feminist and publisher. Douglass ignored his nomination and continued his efforts to win the black vote for Grant.

The value of Douglass's campaigning for Grant's reelection was widely recognized. The *New York Times*, for example, referred to his speeches as "unexcelled among the productions of the campaign." Some political insiders speculated that he would be appointed to the cabinet. Expecting the offer of at least some office, Douglass moved his family to Washington, D.C., during the summer of 1872. Though he had contemplated such a move for some time, its timing was dictated by a disastrous and mysterious fire that destroyed his Rochester home. Taking up residence a short distance from the White House, Douglass waited for political appointment. The wait, however, was in vain. No offers came during Grant's second term.

This was a very trying time for Douglass. Not only did he suffer financial and personal losses in the Rochester fire and the disappointment of being passed over by the administration, he also experienced two costly and embarrassing failures—one of a newspaper, the other a bank.

In 1870 a group of blacks founded a Washington-based newspaper called the *New Era*. Wishing to add the prestige of Douglass's name to this publication, its founders persuaded him to accept the position of corresponding editor. Douglass had no real interest in returning to journalism on a full-time basis. However, he took the job because he felt there was a need for a paper serving the interests of the freedmen. He was also able to get jobs on the paper for his sons Lewis and Frederick, Jr.

From the first the *New Era* was plagued by financial difficulties and within a year it was close to folding. Now publicly associated with the paper, Douglass was loath to see it go under. He bought out the original owners, renamed it the *New National Era*, and turned the day-to-day operation over to his sons. With Douglass's continued financial support and occasional journalistic contributions the *New National Era* survived for a few years. But with the panic of 1873, followed by depression, the paper's finances went quickly from bad to worse. In September 1874, Douglass and his sons published the last issue. Personally, Douglass sustained a loss of more than $10,000.

Some two and a half months before the folding of the *New National Era* Douglass suffered another financial setback as well as damage to his personal reputation when the Freedman's Savings and Trust Company closed its doors. Founded by private investors with a charter from Congress in 1865, the Freedman's Bank hoped to help the newly emancipated slaves learn habits of saving. By 1872 the bank had 32 branches in the Southern states as well as a lavish Washington headquarters. Bad management and unwise loans seriously weakened the bank. The panic of 1873 and subsequent national economic downturn further undermined the bank's solvency.

By the spring of 1874 the bank had a deficit of more than $200,000. The trustees decided to offer the presidency of the bank to Frederick Douglass. Their hope was that his prestige would inspire confidence among black depositors and prevent collapse. Though knowing nothing of the intricacies of banking or of the true state of the bank, personal pride combined with a sense of duty caused Douglass to accept the position. As he later wrote: "So I waked up one morning to find myself seated in a comfortable arm chair, with gold spectacles on my nose, and to hear myself addressed as President of the Freedman's Bank. I could not help reflecting on the contrast between Frederick the slave boy, running about at Col. Lloyd's with only a tow linen shirt to cover him, and Frederick—president of a bank counting its assets by millions. I had heard of golden dreams, but such dreams had no comparison with this reality."

The dream lasted a scant three months. Finding out too late the hopeless condition of the bank, on 20 June 1874 Douglass secured from Congress an act placing the Freedman's Trust in bankruptcy. The depositors recovered later less than 50 percent of the money which they had entrusted to the bank. Certainly Douglass was in no way responsible for the bank's collapse, but not surprisingly much suspicion and blame fell on him. Not since his days in slavery had he experienced such a sense of failure and disgrace. The bank had closed, his paper was about to fold, he had lost much of his own savings, and he had not been given the government appointment that he so much desired.

To make ends meet Douglass returned to the lecture circuit. Lectures were still an extremely popular form of entertainment in post-Civil War America, and throughout the country Lyceum bureaus existed to book and promote speakers. As in antebellum times, Douglass continued to be among the nation's most celebrated orators. However, since slavery was ended and interest in racial issues was on the decline, he found it necessary to speak on other topics. He had lectures on "Folklore of Different Nations," "American Civilization," "The Age of Pictures," "Scandinavian History and Icelandic Sagas," and his most popular talk on "Self-Made Men."

Douglass's drawing power enabled him to charge as much as $200 per speech and with a full lecture schedule he could make a good living. Though he had been lecturing for more than 30 years, he had not lost his ability to captivate audiences. "For ourselves," a reporter noted, "we were constantly astonished at the massiveness of mind, the wonderful accuracy and felicitous use of language, the admirable elocution, and the evidence of intellectual strength and culture that characterized this oration of a man who lived until past twenty years old as a slave, and has since then been mainly self-taught." Another listener called him "one of the world's great orators, and beyond comparison the greatest man of the race yet produced on this continent." Yet though the money was good and the crowds enthusiastic, the hectic pace and the long periods away from home caused the aging Douglass to desire a more settled life.

In 1877 his opportunity came. That year President Rutherford B. Hayes appointed him United States marshal for the District of Columbia. Finally, the political appointment that had so long eluded Douglass had come. As many contemporaries saw it, this honor was "vicarious atonement for the abandonment of the Fifteenth Amendment." While Hayes withdrew the last federal troops from the South, forsaking the former slaves, his appointment of Douglass helped console supporters of black rights.

Douglass, who had previously refused a position from President Johnson, took no apparent notice of those critical of his appointment. To him it was a personal honor and a step forward for his race. He served as marshal from 1877 to 1881. Subsequently President James Garfield appointed him recorder of deeds for the District of Columbia, a post he held from 1881 to 1886. Neither post gave Douglass political power, only money and prestige.

A Washington officeholder at last, Douglass celebrated his new status in 1878 by buying "Cedar Hill," a 15-acre estate with a 20-room Victorian house commanding a view of the capitol and surrounding countryside. Ironically this imposing homestead had once been the property of General Robert E. Lee.

Now in his sixties and very distinguished looking with his full mane of white hair, mustache and beard, Douglass finally had the opportunity to enjoy life. His government duties paid well and left him with much leisure. He was able to read a great deal, perform with the Uniontown Shakespeare club,

Cedar Hall, the imposing residence that Douglass purchased in 1878 and where he died February 20, 1895.

keep up a wide-ranging correspondence, and socialize. At Cedar Hill he entertained frequent visitors. He became skillful at croquet and spent many of his Sunday afternoons playing with young black students from nearby Howard University. Seldom able to enjoy family life in his younger years, now his children and grandchildren were always welcomed and often stayed for long periods.

Douglass's health, which had declined on the lecture circuit, improved at Cedar Hill. He took to walking the five miles from his home to his government office. In 1880 he gave up cigars. But his wife, Anna, who had long suffered from rheumatism, became more sickly. In August of 1882 she died. It had been a long and supportive marriage. Anna had given Douglass her life savings when he first escaped from slavery. She had worked and saved when they had little money. She had always been a fine homemaker and mother. Yet she had never been Douglass's intellectual equal, and the distance between them had grown over the years. While Douglass had continued to mature intellectually and had become one of the major figures of his age, Anna had remained largely illiterate and in the background.

Though never unfaithful to Anna, throughout his married life Douglass had enjoyed the company and friendship of other women. Both black and white women found the tall, handsome, brilliant Douglass very attractive. In white women, such as his close friend Julia Griffiths, he found the intellectual companionship that Anna could not provide. Douglass also liked to be seen in the presence of white women as a way of asserting his equality, even though he knew that any relationship between a black male and a white female rubbed raw the sore of American racial prejudice.

In January 1884, some 18 months after Anna's death, Douglass married Helen Pitts. She was a college-educated white woman who had been Douglass's secretary in the office of the recorder of deeds. When they married she was 46; Douglass was nearly 66.

News of their marriage caused widespread outrage. One southern paper attacked Douglass as "a lecherous old African

Solomon." Blacks and whites alike seemed equally offended. To many blacks the marriage was an insult to Negro womanhood. To most whites it was racially taboo. Even Douglass's sons and daughter openly opposed the marriage.

When asked about the marriage Helen Pitts said simply that "love came to me and I was not afraid to marry the man I loved because of his color." Douglass's answer to the same question was revealing. His first wife, he said, "was the color of my mother, and the second, the color of my father." Indeed, Douglass's own parentage was proof that interracial unions, even though prohibited by law, had been commonplace in slavery. Disapproving of such a union in post-emancipation times was sheer hypocrisy. Throughout his life Douglass rejected any distinctions based on race. In a letter to Elizabeth Cady Stanton, who supported the marriage, he wrote: "I could never have been at peace with my own soul or held up my head among men had I allowed the fear of popular clamor to deter me from following my convictions as to this marriage. I should have gone to my grave a self-accused and self-convicted moral coward."

Helen Pitts, whom Douglass married in January 1884.

Douglass's second marriage was, of course, much more than a blow against racial prejudice. It was a love match. In Helen, Douglass had an intimate who shared many of his intellectual and reformist interests. Both were active in the women's rights movement; they also participated together in literary and theatrical societies. At Cedar Hill they often entertained guests playing music—Helen on piano and Frederick with his violin. Within months the furor over the marriage subsided and from all appearances the couple remained quite happy, never allowing criticisms of their marriage to weaken their affection for one another.

Eighteen eighty-four, the year of Frederick and Helen's wedding, was also an election year, and that November for the first time since before the Civil War a Democrat was elected to the presidency. The new president, Grover Cleveland, allowed Douglass to retain his position as recorder of deeds for more than a year. In 1886, however, Cleveland asked for Douglass's resignation.

No longer employed and with money saved, on 15 September 1886 Douglass and his wife embarked on an extensive tour of Europe. Twice previously Douglass had sailed for England, but on both occasions he was fleeing for safety. Now when he and Helen boarded the Liverpool-bound *City of Rome* he was an internationally renowned dignitary beginning a leisurely grand tour. The couple spent five weeks in England where Douglass renewed old friendships with his former associate, Julia Griffiths, and with Anna and Ellen Richardson, the women who had negotiated the purchase of his freedom some 39 years before.

From Great Britain they traveled on to France. Their extended stay in Paris was made pleasant because the Douglasses were guided to many points of interest by two American expatriots and friends, Theodore Stanton, the son of Elizabeth Cady Stanton, and Theodore Tilton. From Paris they took an unhurried tour through southern France and Italy. Then on February 13, 1887, they sailed for Egypt. While there the 69-year-old Douglass even managed, with the help of some younger Arab guides, to climb to the top of Cheops, the highest of the pyramids. Their return trip took them to Greece and then once again through Italy and France. In Paris, Helen learned that her mother was ill and arrangements were made for her return voyage. She sailed for home that June. Douglass, because of previous commitments, went on to visit friends and give talks in Great Britain. Missing Helen and his home he returned to the United States in August 1887. It had been an unforgettable trip filled with memorable historic and artistic sights and warm friendships. Douglass also found once again that in Europe he could "walk the world unquestioned, a man among men," with no color discrimination.

Back home it was not long before he was once more involved in Republican politics. Present at the June 1888 Republican Convention in Chicago, Douglass urged the delegates to adopt a platform pledging protection for "the black citizen." Influenced by the black leader, the party did advocate federal support of black voting rights. Pleased at this, Douglass readily accepted when the Republican National Committee asked him "to make as many speeches as you will find it within your ability to do" on behalf of the party's presidential candidate, Benjamin Harrison.

Helped by Douglass's campaigning and the black vote, Harrison was elected. On taking office in 1889 he offered the aging ex-slave an appointment as minister-resident and consul-general to the Republic of Haiti. Douglass was honored by this unsolicited offer. He had long admired Haiti, the first free black republic in the Western Hemisphere. Some friends expressed fears that he was too old and that the tropical climate would be bad for his health. Others argued that his leadership was needed in the United States. Despite these concerns Douglass accepted the appointment. He and Helen departed from Washington in September 1889.

From the outset this diplomatic mission was troubled. Haiti was a small, proud, and highly unstable black nation. Just before the Douglasses arrival there a new government headed by President Modestin Hyppolite had taken power by a violent overthrow of the former president, François Légitime.

Hyppolite's success was due largely to his support by the United States and the presence of American naval vessels in Haitian waters at the time of the coup d'état. The United States now expected to receive concessions from the new government. However, anti-American feeling was strong in Haiti and the Hyppolite government knew that any special deals with the United States could lead to revolution.

Specifically the U.S. wanted Douglass to obtain a lease of Môle St. Nicolas, a port at Haiti's northwest tip. To protect American interests in the Caribbean, the United States at this time desired the port as a naval base and coaling station. One reason Douglass had been selected for minister was because the Harrison administration assumed that the well-known black leader would be more trusted than a white diplomat in negotiations with the Haitians.

Though Douglass did not oppose American expansionism, he did have far more respect for the Haitian people and their sovereignty than did most American officials. Perhaps sensing this, the Harrison administration took negotiations out of his hands by placing Admiral Bancroft Gherardi in charge. Unfortunately the admiral relied more on the power of the American fleet than diplomatic finesse. After months of negotiations in April 1891 the Haitian government rejected the American request for the lease, stating that "Haiti could not enter negotiations without appearing to yield to foreign pressure."

Douglass had previously warned Secretary of State James Blaine that the American naval presence was causing feelings "of apprehension, anxiety and even of alarm." He was in no way responsible for the failure of negotiations. Much of the American press, however, did blame him, some even charging that his color made him identify with Haitian rather than American interests. Furious, Douglass returned to Washington. On July 30, 1891, he resigned as minister, stating "personal considerations" as reason.

The Haitian government and people were resentful over the Môle incident but refused to fault the American minister. After Douglass's resignation letters poured in lamenting the fact that he would not be returning to Haiti. One letter signed by 23 members of the Haitian College called Douglass "one of the greatest champions of liberty, justice and equality."

Two years later in 1893, the Haitian government appointed Douglass as Haitian Commissioner at the World's Columbian Exposition at Chicago. To Douglass this was a great honor. In fact he would be the only Afro-American to have an official role in this world's fair. Not even a black guide or guard had been appointed by the exposition's organizers.

In his speech opening the Haitian Pavilion on January 2, 1893, Douglass paid tribute to Haiti. Until blacks there struck a blow for freedom, he argued, "the Christian world slept profoundly over slavery." Haiti "has grandly served the cause of universal liberty. We should not forget that the freedom you and I enjoy today; that the freedom that eight hundred thousand colored people enjoy in the British West Indies; the freedom that has come to the colored race the world over, is largely due to the brave stand taken by the black sons of Haiti ninety years ago." Freedom for Haiti, Douglass stressed, "*was not given as a boon, but conquered as a right!* Her people fought for it."

To Douglass, Haiti had served not only as the fountainhead of black freedom but would continue to stand as the symbol of black hope. Though ostracized by white nations for most of its history, Douglass reminded his audience that "Haiti still lives. . . . I will not, I cannot believe that her star is to go out in darkness, but I will rather believe that whatever may happen of peace or war Haiti will remain in the firmament of nations, and, like the star of the north, will shine on and shine on forever."

11

THE LAST YEARS

When Douglass resigned his position as minister to Haiti in 1891 he was 73 years old and had been a Republican officeholder for most of the preceding decade and a half. During those years his fame and fortune had reached new heights. He was invited to speak at prominent national and local meetings. Senators, congressmen, and even presidents consulted and socialized with him. Dignitaries and ordinary citizens of both races sought him out at Cedar Hill. Abroad he was treated as if he were a nobleman or a great chieftain, while in the United States he was recognized as the preeminent leader of black America.

Aware of the value his life story had as an example for his race and a legacy to history, in 1881 he produced an expanded and updated version of his autobiography. Published as *Life and Times of Frederick Douglass*, he again updated and revised this work in a final edition in 1892. Like a black Ben Franklin, Douglass presented his public life as a success story, a triumph over adversity, and as a model for Negro America.

Yet while Douglass's personal fortunes were on the rise during the late nineteenth century, the lot of most black Americans was hitting a new low. Following the final withdrawal of federal troops from the South conditions for blacks had gone from bad to worse. By force, economic intimidation, and unfair election laws, Southern Negroes were systematically deprived of the vote. Black labor was exploited through a tenant and sharecropping system that kept blacks perpetually in bondage to white land- and storeowners. In all phases of life, segregation of the races became the rule. Any black daring to challenge this American system of apartheid was in danger of physical assault or lynching.

Through these years Douglass had raised his voice against the retreat from Reconstruction and the revival of racism. Yet as an optimist he could not bring himself to believe that the oppression experienced by most blacks was permanent. To him progress was inevitable, despite temporary setbacks. Celebrity status and material comfort had made Douglass more complacent. Living the good life at Cedar Hill, associating largely with upper- and middle-class whites, he had distanced himself from the life of suffering that most Southern blacks endured. He continued to believe that despite racism any Negro could succeed through hard work and moral character just as he had. This Horatio Alger fantasy of the self-made man blinded Douglass to the systematic nature of black oppression. He should have known better. Even his own children and their families, despite many advantages, were unable to succeed and remained dependent on Douglass.

He also had too much faith in the Republican party. To Douglass that party would always mean Lincoln and Sumner, emancipation and the Fifteenth Amendment. He tried to serve as the party's conscience and to call it back to the ideals of the Civil War and Reconstruction. He was slow to realize that Republicans had grown indifferent to black rights and had come to terms with the white South. It was not that Douglass was entirely naive about this. He and other blacks were in a political bind. There was, they believed, no viable alternative to the Republican party for blacks. With that party at least there was always the hope that the old egalitarian ideals could be revived, that somehow the legacy of the Civil War for blacks—freedom, citizenship, suffrage, and justice—could be saved.

But while Douglass had become more moderate as a Republican and an officeholder, he never resigned himself to acceptance of white supremacy. In his last years he became more aware of the duplicity of the Republican party and of the pervasiveness of white racism. "The tide of popular prejudice" against blacks, he lamented in 1884, had "swollen by a thousand streams" since the war.

Upon his return from Europe in 1888, Douglass made his first trip into the deep South. His travels through South Carolina and Georgia were a shocking revelation. In a Washington speech soon after this Southern visit he called emancipation "a stupendous fraud." In words reminiscent of his earlier antislavery oratory he condemned the sharecropping system that held blacks in a state of poverty and powerlessness. The black man "struggles and struggles, but, like a man in a morass, the more he struggles the deeper he sinks." Douglass denounced the national government for having left the Negro "a deserted, a defrauded, a swindled, and an outcast man—in law, free; in fact, a slave." For blacks, he claimed, "every attribute of a just government is contradicted." The government "demands allegiance, but denies protection. . . . It imposes upon him all the burdens of citizenship and withholds from him all its benefits."

By the time Douglass resigned as minister to Haiti in 1891, his disappointment with Republicans was obvious. "The Republican party," he sadly noted, "is converted into a party of money, rather than a party of humanity and justice." Now in his mid-seventies and no longer seeking office, he turned his attention to the most heinous crime committed against blacks: lynching.

During Reconstruction the Klan and other white vigilante groups had used violence against blacks as a way of regaining political power. By the beginning of the 1890s white supremacy was everywhere triumphant in the South; nowhere were blacks a political threat. Nevertheless the racist violence of which they were victims continued and grew. There was an alarming increase of white mobs lynching black men. Hundreds of blacks yearly were hanged, shot, mutilated, or even burned to death for the alleged crime of raping or attempting to rape white women.

In point of fact there was no epidemic of rape in the South by blacks or whites. But by raising the specter of vengeful blacks threatening the purity of white womanhood, whites were able to gain public sympathy and take people's minds off the real crime of lynching. In effect the victims of white violence were being made to appear bestial and therefore deserving of the lynch mob's brutality. In this Victorian age white fears of sexual assault by a black male against a white female were commonplace even though actual cases were virtually nonexistent. Consequently many well-meaning Northerners who might ordinarily have been sympathetic to the plight of Southern blacks expressed little concern over the rampant lynchings. In fact many Northerners came to agree with Southern white supremacists who charged that blacks were unfit for voting and other citizenship rights. Talk of colonization also revived.

All of this alarmed the aged Douglass. It appeared that his dream of creating a truly color-blind national community had failed. The evil of racial prejudice had not been routed. Racism had survived the antislavery crusade, the Civil War, and Reconstruction. Now in the last years of the nineteenth century it was everywhere, symbolized most blatantly by the rampaging white lynch mobs.

While whites in the civil-rights struggle remained silent, Douglass took up the issue of lynching with the same vehemence he had displayed more than a generation previous in the cause of abolition. Perhaps being married to a white woman made him particularly sensitive to the sexual aspect of the issue. Certainly he realized the hypocrisy and falsehood of the charges against blacks.

Accompanied by Mary Church Terrell, a young black reformer, Douglass visited President Harrison in an effort to win support for a federal anti-lynching law. Though Douglass made an eloquent plea, Harrison refused to take up the cause. Douglass then took his message to the nation in a series of lectures and articles. "Not a breeze comes to us from the late rebellious states," he wrote, "that is not tainted and freighted with Negro blood." In 1894, in what was to be one of his last great lectures and pamphlets, "The Lesson of the Hour: Why the Negro is Lynched," he condemned not only lynching, but the entire system of black oppression.

"We claim to be a highly civilized and Christian country," he began. "I fearlessly affirm that there is nothing in the history of savages to surpass the blood-chilling horrors and fiendish excesses perpetrated against the colored people of this country, by the so-called enlightened people of the South." The charge of "assaults upon white women," he pointed out, was only a new excuse "to degrade the Negro" and to pave the way "for his entire disfranchisement as an American citizen." Nor did he blame only the ignorant lower-class whites who composed the rank-and-file of mobs: "the upper classes of the South seem to be in full sympathy." These men of "wealth and respectability" were the real cause of "the mob and its deeds."

The press and much of the public had begun referring to Southern violence against blacks as "the Negro Problem." To Douglass this was the "old trick of misnaming things." "There is nothing the matter with the Negro, whatever," he argued; "he is all right. Learned or ignorant, he is all right. He is neither a lyncher, a mobocrat or an anarchist. He is now what he has ever been, a loyal, law-abiding, hard working and peaceable man." By calling injustice to blacks, "the Negro Problem," one "removes the burden of proof from the old master class and imposes it on the Negro. It puts upon the race a work which belongs to the nation." It places "the fault at the door of the Negro and removes it from the door of the white man, shields the guilty and blames the innocent, makes the Negro responsible, when it should so make the nation."

The problem, Douglass concluded, was not a Negro problem but a "national problem" caused by racial prejudice. Disfranchisement of blacks was no answer, nor was colonization. The solution was one of simple justice, of protecting citizens from fraud and violence, of compelling obedience to the Constitution. "If this were done there would be no Negro problem or national problem to vex the South or to vex the nation."

The crusade against lynching proved to be Frederick Douglass's last great fight. He did not succeed, but his ringing pleas for justice foreshadowed the momentous civil rights struggles of the twentieth century.

On February 20, 1895, Douglass spent much of the day attending a meeting of the National Council of Women in Washington. He had continued his support of women's rights throughout his later years. Indeed, 10 years earlier he had confided to a friend that he found women's rights gatherings "a substitute for the old time anti-slavery meetings." Shortly after five P.M. Douglass returned to Cedar Hill. There while talking of the women's meeting with Helen he collapsed. He died quickly of a heart attack. He was 77 years old, though he had never known his exact age. Slavery had denied him a birth date. He had lived to see that institution abolished and the rights of his people enshrined in the Constitution. He had also been the sad witness to the increasing violation of those constitutional rights in the last years of his life.

When news of Douglass's death reached the delegates of the National Council of Women at the opening of the evening session, Mary Wright Sewall, the presiding officer, before adjourning the meeting in tribute, told the hushed crowd:

> Surely it will be regarded as an historic coincidence that the man who, in his own person, embodied the history of almost a century, in the struggle between freedom and oppression, should have spent his last day as a witness of the united efforts of those who have come . . . to demand a new expression of freedom in the relation of woman to the world, to society, and to the state.

Throughout the United States and Europe the death of America's greatest black leader made headlines. Thousands of obituaries and testimonials praised his extraordinary career. Elizabeth Cady Stanton called Douglass "the only man I ever saw who understood the degradation of the disenfranchisement of women." An obituary in the London *Daily News* stated: "from first to last his was a noble life. His own people have lost a father and a friend, and all good men have lost a comrade in the fight for the legal emancipation of one race and the spiritual emancipation of all."

But perhaps the most fitting tribute came from black activist Rosa Hazard Hazel. In a speech entitled "The Standard By Which Douglass' Greatness Shall Be Determined" she suggested "that future biographers may think that the greatness of Douglass lay not alone in a life-long consecration for the elevation of his race, but in the breadth of view of this man of the people, who reached out not only for the good of the Negro race, but . . . [for] that kind of justice which ignores both race and sex, giving to all equal opportunities, obligations and incentives. . . ."

Henry Wilson, Grant's vice president, once wrote of Douglass that "his life is in itself an epic which finds few to equal it in the realms of either romance or reality." This would seem a strong claim to make for most people's lives; in Douglass's case, however, it was true. Born in 1818 as Frederick Bailey, a Maryland slave with little knowledge of his mother and less of his father, he educated himself, daringly escaped from slavery, and went on to lead a long and productive life as an abolitionist, reformer, orator, newspaper editor, writer, political leader, and government official. Driven by his love of freedom, Douglass played a major role in the liberation of his people and the transformation of the nation. He died free; he died honored.

Like Lincoln, Douglass would leave a legacy in death: the ideal of freedom for all people. He had fought to create a nation in which character, and not color or sex, would determine a person's status. A great American had died; his vision still lives on.

SUGGESTED ADDITIONAL READINGS

Those interested in examining further the life of Frederick Douglass should begin by reading the three versions of his autobiography: *The Narrative of the Life of Frederick Douglass* (1845), *My Bondage and My Freedom* (1855), and *The Life and Times of Frederick Douglass* (rev. ed. 1892). Of the three, the original *Narrative* is by far the most powerful and influential, though the latter volumes bring Douglass's story forward in time and include subtle but revealing changes in the story of his life as a slave. These autobiographies uncover much about the institution of slavery, and reveal Douglass's perception of his own life as a role model for blacks. While there are no glaring errors of fact in these volumes, they offer less than the full truth. Douglass was very guarded about his personal life. He also was writing for a purpose. The first two autobiographies clearly were written to serve the antislavery cause. The last volume was aimed at setting the historical record straight and assuring that the black leader's legacy to his race and nation was understood. For a fascinating analysis of how Douglass created his life in the autobiographies, see Peter F. Walker, *Moral Choices: Memory, Desire, and Imagination in Nineteenth Century American Abolition* (1978).

The best collection of Douglass's writings other than the autobiographies is Philip S. Foner, ed., *The Life and Writings of Frederick Douglass* (5 vols., 1950–1975). Yale University Press, under the editorship of John W. Blassingame, is in the process of publishing what promises to be the definitive edition of Douglass's writings. To date the first three volumes of Series I of *The Frederick Douglass Papers* (1979, 1982, 1987) have been issued. An excellent one-volume anthology of Douglass's writings is: Michael Meyer, ed., *Frederick Douglass: The Narrative and Selected Writings* (1984).

There are two standard full-length biographies of Douglass: Benjamin Quarles, *Frederick Douglass* (1948), and Philip S. Foner, *Frederick Douglass* (1964). The latter volume collects the biographical material from the first four volumes of Foner's *Life and Writings of Frederick Douglass* and was originally published from 1950 to 55. Both of these studies are well researched, thorough, and informative. Both also have defects. For one thing they are dated. Slavery, Northern free blacks, abolitionists and the unique role of black abolitionists, John Brown, Republican ideology, the coming of the Civil War, Lincoln, and radical Reconstruction are among the major topics relating to Douglass's life that have undergone significant reinterpretation since Quarles's and Foner's books appeared.

A second problem is that both Quarles and Foner accept too uncritically the self-image that Douglass presents in his three autobiographies. Neither author seriously examines the more personal conflicts and crises of Douglass's life. Finally, both authors can be faulted for using Douglass for their own purposes. Benjamin Quarles, a black historian writing in the years of World War II and the early Cold War, presented Douglass as a black Horatio Alger able to win a respectable place in society. For Philip Foner, a white Marxist writing during the McCarthy period, Douglass was a revolutionary prophet of racial equality and radical class consciousness. Both authors, in other words, portray an exemplary Douglass as an exponent of their own ideals.

More recent Douglass scholarship has helped make possible an assessment of Douglass's life less dictated by either ideology or the autobiographies. Two of the best examples are Dickson J. Preston's *Young Frederick Douglass: The Maryland Years* (1980) and Waldo E. Martin, Jr.'s, *The Mind of Frederick Douglass* (1984). Preston's careful research in the plantation and country records of Talbot County, Maryland, reveals a great deal of new information about Douglass's early life and his family. Martin's study is a first-rate piece of intellectual history. His detailed analysis of Douglass's thought reveals a complex and sometimes contradictory mind.

Also valuable are some of the recent unpublished doctoral dissertations on Douglass. The best of these include: David W. Blight, "Keeping Faith in Jubilee: Frederick Douglass and the Meaninig of the Civil War," (University of Wisconsin-Madison, 1985, forthcoming as a book), an examination of the impact of the war on Douglass's life and thought; William Lloyd Van Deburg, "Rejected of Men: The Changing Religious Views of William Lloyd Garrison and Frederick Douglass," (Michigan State University, 1973), a study that traces the religious evolution of these two great abolitionists; and Leslie F. Goldstein, "The Political Thought of Frederick Douglass," (Cornell University, 1974), a fine study of the changes in Douglass's ideology.

Useful articles on aspects of Douglass's career include: August Meier, "Frederick Douglass' Vision for America: A Case Study in Nineteenth-Century Negro Protest," in Harold M. Hyman and Leonard W. Levy, eds., *Freedom and Reform* (1967); Jane and William Pease, "Boston Garrisonians and Frederick Douglass," *Canadian Journal of History*, 2 (September 1967), 29-48; David W. Blight, "Frederick Douglass and the American Apocolypse," *Civil War History*, 31 (December 1985), 309-328; Stephen M. Weissman, "Frederick Douglass," *Psychoanalytic Study of the Child*, 25 (1975), 725-51; Louis H. Gates, Jr., "Frederick Douglass and the Language of the Self," *Yale Review*, 70 (Summer 1981), 592-611; Gerald Fulkerson, "Exile as Emergence: Frederick Douglass in Great Britain, 1845-1847," *Quarterly Journal of Speech*, 60 (February 1974), 69-82; William L. Van Deburg, "Frederick Douglass: Maryland Slave to Religious Liberal," *Maryland History Magazine*, 69 (Spring 1974), 27-43; Leslie F. Goldstein, "Violence as an Instrument for Social Change: The Views of Frederick Douglass," *Journal of Negro History*, 61 (January 1976), 61-72; and Christopher Breiseth, "Lincoln and Frederick Douglass: Another Debate," *Illinois State Historical Society Journal*, 68 (1975), 9-26.

There are two recent biographies of Douglass, though neither replaces the earlier works of Quarles and Foner. Arna Bontemps, *Free at Last: The Life of Frederick Douglass* (1971) is well written, but not analytical. Nathan Irvin Huggins's *Slave and Citizen: The Life of Frederick Douglass* (1980) is often insightful, but sketchy.

Of books on slavery the most helpful for the student of Douglass is Kenneth M. Stampp, *The Peculiar Institution* (1957). Gilbert Osofsky, ed., *Puttin' On Ole Master* (1969) is a collection of slave narratives by Henry Bibb, William Wells Brown, and Solomon Northrup useful for comparison with Douglass's classic *Narrative*.

Two overviews of abolitionism are: James Brewer Stewart, *Holy Warriors: The Abolitionists and American Slavery* (1976), and Merton Dillon, *The Abolitionists: The Growth of a Dissenting Minority* (1973). Benjamin Quarles's *The Black Abolitionists* (1969) is a good introduction to that subject. Also valuable are: Jane and William Pease, *They Who Would Be Free: Blacks' Search for Freedom, (1831-1861* (1974), and Vincent Harding, *There Is a River: The Black Struggle for Freedom in America* (1981).

Douglas T. Miller's *The Birth of Modern America, 1820-1850* (1970) and *Then Was the Future: The North in the Age of Jackson, 1815-1850* (1973) describe the North at the time of Douglass's escape to that region. The only study of free blacks in the North is Leon Litwack's *North of Slavery: The Negro in the Free States, 1790-1860* (1961). Free blacks in the South are the subject of Ira Berlin's *Slaves Without Masters* (1974).

Philip S. Foner, ed., *Frederick Douglass on Women's Rights* (1976) is a collection of Douglass's writings on that issue. Lois W. Banner, *Elizabeth Cady Stanton* (1980) is a fine brief biography of that important feminist. A good general study of the women's movement is Eleanor Flexner, *Century of Struggle* (1959).

Douglass's relationship with John Brown is explored in: Stephen B. Oates, *To Purge This Land With Blood* (1984 ed.); Richard O. Boyer, *The Legend of John Brown* (1973); John Anthony Scott and Robert Alan Scott, *John Brown of Harper's*

Ferry (1988); and Benjamin Quarles, *Allies for Freedom: Blacks and John Brown* (1974).

Eric Foner's *Free Soil, Free Labor, Free Men* (1970) is an excellent study of the rise of the Republican party and its ideology. Two articles exploring Lincoln's attitudes toward slavery and blacks are: Don E. Fehrenbacher, "Only His Stepchildren: Lincoln and the Negro," *Civil War History*, XX (December 1974), 293-310, and George M. Fredrickson, "A Man but Not a Brother: Abraham Lincoln and Racial Equality," *The Journal of Southern History*, XLI (February 1975), 39-58. Also valuable on this topic are: LaWanda Cox, *Lincoln and Black Freedom* (1981) and Benjamin Quarles, *Lincoln and the Negro* (1962).

James M. McPherson's *The Struggle for Quality: Abolitionists and the Negro in the Civil War and Reconstruction* (1964) helps place Douglass's concerns during the war and Reconstruction into a larger perspective. Other useful works for the postwar years include: Leon Litwack, *Been in the Storm So Long: The Aftermath of Slavery* (1979); Stanley P. Hirshson, *Farewell to the Bloody Shirt: Northern Republicans and the Southern Negro, 1877-1893* (1962); Rayford W. Logan, *The Betrayal of the Negro* (1965); and W.E.B. DuBois's classic *Black Reconstruction, 1860-1880* (1935).

Finally Douglass's brief period as minister to Haiti is treated in Rayford W. Logan, *The Diplomatic Relations of the United States with Haiti, 1776-1891* (1941).

INDEX